BRIDAL GUIDE®
MAGAZINE'S

New Etiquette
for
Today's Bride

BRIDAL GUIDE®
MAGAZINE'S

New Etiquette
~ for ~
Today's Bride

DIANE FORDEN, EDITOR IN CHIEF
WITH KRISTEN FINELLO

WARNER BOOKS

NEW YORK   BOSTON

Warner Books, Inc., 1271 Avenue of the Americas, New York, NY 10020

Visit our Web site at www.twbookmark.com.

A LifeTime Media Production
LifeTime Media Inc.
352 Seventh Avenue, 15th Floor
New York, NY 10001

Printed in the United States of America

First Paperback Printing: January 2005
10 9 8 7 6 5 4 3 2 1

ISBN: 0-446-67822-8
LCCN: 2004114821

Cover design by Claire Brown

Contents

Introduction

Congratulations! Now that you're a newly minted bride-to-be, you're probably feeling a flood of emotions—from elated to excited to overwhelmed. Perhaps you've dreamt of your wedding day for years, or maybe you never gave a thought to white dresses or caterers before you slipped on an engagement ring. Either way, your head is probably spinning with all the decisions you'll have to make in the next few months: Do you want a large wedding or a small one? Traditional or offbeat? Near home or at a special destination? And those are just for starters!

For the sake of your sanity, we'll let you in on a little secret right now: Planning your wedding is one of the most enjoyable things you'll do in life, but it can also be pretty stressful. Many of us picture the Hollywood version of the bride-to-be: a carefree gal who glides through life sampling sweet desserts, trying on beautiful gowns and being feted at endless parties in her honor. You'll definitely get to do all that—we promise! But if you're like most of today's brides you'll have to sandwich your cake tastings and dress fittings between work and your other commitments, which can make for a hectic few months. And that's where this etiquette book comes in—it will help you navigate the process of wedding planning easily and efficiently.

What Etiquette *Really* Is

First of all, don't be fooled by the "E" word. Etiquette isn't about being stuffy and super-formal, rather it's about respecting everyone involved in your big day—from parents to guests to service providers—to ensure that your engagement and wedding aren't overshadowed by any ruffled feathers or budding family feuds.

In the pages of this book, you'll find realistic answers to your most pressing etiquette questions and practical advice addressing your biggest concerns, like how to handle divorced parents who can't stand each other, inform guests their little darlings aren't invited to the wedding, word invitations properly, handle gift-giving with grace, register for gifts, and much more.

21st-Century Twists

As you're reading this book, keep in mind that etiquette is based on tradition but has evolved over the years to embrace new customs and practices. In other words, the strict rules of how things "should" be done that your mother and grandmother followed to the letter may not apply to you at all! Did you know, for instance, that a white dress isn't only for a first-time bride anymore, or that the groom's best man can be a woman? In this book, you'll get the latest scoop on these and many other issues.

Let's Get Going

Okay, it's almost time to turn you loose and let you start planning your ideal wedding ceremony and reception. But before you jump head first into this crazy time, we thought we'd share just a few things you can expect to experience over the next weeks and months. Don't be surprised if

...your vocabulary grows by leaps and bounds as you add previously unknown words and phrases like fondant, wishing well, and Jack-and-Jill shower (no, it's not as risqué as it sounds!) to your conversations.

...your moods alternate fast and furiously between utter bliss ("I am so in love!") to sheer frustration ("What do you mean this bridesmaid dress isn't available in crimson?!?!").

...you, who easily made decisions like where to go to college and which jobs to apply for, agonize over choices like fondant (there's that word again!) versus butter cream frosting.

But rest assured: At the end of this wild ride called engagement, you will make a stunning bride. And you'll be able to look back on your wedding fondly, because it will be a wonderful day.

Ready to dive in and start creating your dream celebration? Great! Take a deep breath, and let the planning begin.

1

Getting Engaged

It's official: You're getting married! And if you're like most women, once you were finally able to tear your eyes away from your fiancé and the newly placed ring on your left hand, your first thought was: "I can't wait to tell people!" Whether you immediately whipped out your cell phone to speed-dial your best friend or made a surprise visit to your parents' house to show off your rock, you probably realized that there are a lot of people who will want to hear about your engagement.

Start Spreading the News

If you haven't already, now's the time to start sharing your exciting news with the world—or at least your own special corner of the world. The first to hear the big announcement? That honor should go to your immediate families. Your parents and your fiancé's parents, as well as any children either of you have from previous relationships, should be told before anyone else. (If you have children, tell them alone—without your fiancé present—so they have time to digest the news and ask you questions.) Tradition calls for the bride's parents to learn of the engagement first, and then the groom's. But what if your parents or your fiancé's are divorced? You can inform one parent and then the other right after. That way, one parent doesn't find out much later than the other.

Spreading the word of your upcoming "I do's" to those closest to you—parents, siblings, and grandparents —is best done face-to-face. If your families are close by, it's fun to put a bottle of bubbly on ice and invite them over for cake and champagne when you make your announcement, or you can arrange a time to stop by their homes. If your folks or your groom-to-be's don't live nearby, now would be the perfect time to schedule a weekend visit. If your fiancé went the ultra-traditional route and informed your father of his intention to propose, then your parents will have a heads-up on the announcement. Still, visiting them with your new fiancé is a nice gesture. No doubt they'll want to celebrate with the two of you in person.

Once both sets of parents know of your engagement, it's nice to get them together for introductions. Tradition suggests that the mother of the groom calls the mother of the bride to relay her congratulations and extend an invitation to meet (getting together for brunch, dinner, or drinks are all good options). But that rule has been relaxed in recent years, and now it's perfectly fine for your mom to make the first move if she doesn't hear from your groom's mother within a few weeks. If your parents live too far apart to get together—say your parents live in San Antonio and his reside in Seattle—then a note from one mother to the other saying how pleased she is about the upcoming marriage is a thoughtful gesture.

When it comes to informing other family members and friends, you can either do it in person or over the telephone. E-mail is also acceptable these days. With your boss or coworkers, sharing the news face-to-face makes the most sense since you presumably see one another on a daily basis. If you work closely with colleagues in another location, though, phone or e-mail are equally effective.

Stop the Presses! I'm Getting Married!

Many couples choose to announce their engagement publicly in their local newspaper. This is a smart way to spread the news to a large number of people, since sending printed announcement cards is inappropriate. (Printed announcements should only be used to announce a wedding, not an engagement. For information on sending wedding announcements, see chapter 3: "Invitations and Wedding Announcements.") Newspaper announcements usually run two to three months prior to the wedding, but they can be published up to a year in advance. Consider placing your announcement in your and your fiancé's hometown papers, as well as the papers that serve the community in which you now live. Don't forget to include your engagement news in any alumni and professional publications that publish milestone announcements as well. Hold off on publishing your announcement, though, if either you or your fiancé is still legally married to another person (even if a divorce is pending), if either of you have had a very recent death in the family, or if an immediate family member is gravely ill.

How to Get Your Announcement Published

If the last time your name was in the local paper was when your high school softball team won the championship or you made the honor roll, it's time to brush up on what it takes to get your name in print. Since the requirements for engagement announcements vary by publication, you'll need to check with your paper to find out exactly what you need to do. (At many papers, the lifestyle editor is the person to contact.) Some newspapers provide an announcement form that you simply fill in and submit. Other papers give you more leeway to create your own announcement (read on for hints on how to do that), and still others give you the option of using their form or writing it yourself.

Also, find out if an engagement photo can be printed along with your announcement. Traditionally, an engagement photo was a solo portrait of the bride, but these days a couple shot is common. Some wedding photographers include a sitting for an engagement photo in their wedding packages. If yours doesn't (or if you haven't yet booked a photographer), it's perfectly fine to submit another good-quality, close-up photograph. Whether you go the professional or do-it-yourself route, be sure to check with your newspaper about any photo requirements. For example, does the picture you submit have to be a certain size? Are black and white or color both acceptable? Do you need a print of the photo or can you send the image digitally? Don't forget to find out ahead of time whether or not you can expect to have your photo returned. (Some papers instruct you to send a self-addressed stamped envelope if you want your photo back; others don't return photos at all.) Finally, inquire about any costs associated with your engagement announcement. Many newspapers run them gratis, but others charge a fee.

Writing Your Announcement

If your newspaper doesn't have a standard form, or if you choose not to use it, you'll have to craft your own prose. Not a writer?

Don't panic. Engagement announcements are pretty standard. Shorter ones contain just basic information such as where each of you went to school and where you work. More detailed versions can get into where your parents work and live, and so on. Ready to begin? Take a look at the samples below for an idea of how announcements are usually written. Then check out Appendix A in this book to see how to word your announcement to add any special information that you'd like to include (graduate degrees, for example).

One final tip: Don't forget to include your street address, phone number, and e-mail address with the text of your announcement in case the newspaper staff needs to contact you for more information. You can even copy or tear out one of the forms in the appendix and use it to submit your announcement information.

Who Should Announce Your Engagement?

Your official engagement announcement can be made by your parents or by you and your fiancé. Some couples choose to announce their own engagement if they are hosting their own wedding or if they are older (and perhaps have been married before) and have been independent of their parents for some time. If both of your parents are deceased, a close relative such as a sibling, grandparent, aunt, or uncle can fill in.

Here's an example of how the traditional wording works:

Mr. and Mrs. Kenneth Johnson of Cambridge, Massachusetts, announce the engagement of their daughter, Suzanne Marie Johnson, to Scott Thompson, son of Mr. and Mrs. Robert Thompson of Albuquerque, New Mexico.
A May wedding has been planned.

Customizing Your Announcement for Special Situations

Depending on your individual circumstances, you may want to modify the wording above. To find out how to phrase your announcement to suit other situations, like divorced or deceased parents or a second marriage, see Appendix A.

Can We Talk?

Q: We just got engaged, but our wedding won't be for another two years. What's the most appropriate way to share our news?

Erin, 31, Pennsylvania

A: Congratulations! No doubt you're so excited about your engagement that you want to shout the news from rooftops! While actually shouting from rooftops is out (but you already knew that), spreading the news by word of mouth *is* the best way to go. Why? With your wedding still two years away, it's too early for a printed newspaper announcement—those typically appear just several months to a year before your wedding. For now, enjoy telling your family, friends, and coworkers about your engagement in person, via e-mail, or by sending a handwritten note. Good news travels fast, so once you inform those folks they'll probably happily pass the information on to everyone they know.

Engagement Party Etiquette

Once word of your newly betrothed status is out, friends and family may ask if you're planning an engagement party. Whether or not to have one is completely up to you and your families. While it's not required, it can be a fun way for members of the bridal party and both families to get to know each other before the wedding. When it comes to hosting the shindig, just about any friend or relative can step up, but traditionally it is the bride's parents who do the honors. If your families really love to party and more than one engagement bash is scheduled, the party thrown by your parents (if there is one) should take place before any others.

Engagement bashes can be as formal or casual as you choose. Some popular options: an evening cocktail party, a brunch or lunch buffet at a favorite restaurant, or a cookout at home. You can even throw a surprise engagement party, where you can tell non-immediate friends and family your news. How

Avoiding Gift Gaffes

Your engagement party will likely be the first of many occasions at which you receive presents from well-wishers, but remember: Gifts are not required, so be tactful in handling the ones you receive so guests who didn't bring presents don't feel awkward. You'll be a gift star with these tips:

Do register for gifts before your engagement party, and let your immediate family and close friends know what store(s) you choose. They can pass that information on to guests who ask. But only if they ask!

Don't include registry information with your engagement party invitation—or in the wedding invitation itself. The only place that is appropriate is in a bridal shower invitation.

Do hold off on opening gifts until after the festivities, if not everyone has brought a gift. Opening presents in front of your guests will just embarrass those who didn't bring something.

Don't forget to send a handwritten thank-you note promptly for each gift you receive.

it works: The host (say, you or your parents) sends out the invitations without revealing the true reason for the celebration. Once all the guests have arrived, gather everyone for your big announcement: We're engaged! For a regular, non-surprise get-together, the invitations should specify that the event is an engagement party. At some point during the evening, the host—often the father of the bride—should propose a toast to the to-be-wed couple. One other thing to keep in mind: When reviewing the guest list, be sure that you are only inviting people you plan to invite to the wedding.

Choosing Your Bridal Party

Another important task during your engagement is selecting the members of your bridal party, the people most dear to you (think of them as the MVPs of your life) who will have an important role in your wedding. In your just-got-engaged excitement, it's tempting to rush out and start lining up a bunch of bridesmaids and groomsmen, but it's wise to take a few days or weeks (depending on how soon you plan to tie the knot) to carefully consider your choices. After all, if you run into a high school pal in the mall and blurt out an invitation to join your wedding party just because you're happy to see her, there's no socially correct way to "un-ask" her when you come to your senses later on! (Hey, it's happened!)

Bright Idea

Is Mom the most important woman in your life? Ask her to be your matron of honor. Many brides today are doing this because they're among the generation of daughters who became "pals" with their moms.

Personalizing Your Picks

The good news about choosing your 'maids and men: The old rules that once dictated who could stand up for you are no longer written in stone. Gender alone, for example, doesn't determine whether someone makes the cut to join the bride's side or the groom's side.

	TRADITIONAL	TODAY
Maid or Matron of Honor	This role usually falls to the bride's sister or close female friend or relative.	A sister, dear girlfriend, or female relative, while still popular choices, aren't the only options. If the bride's best pal is a guy, he can act as the "man of honor" or "male of honor." Do you have two sisters or friends you're equally close with? There's no need to choose between them. Instead, ask them to share this honored position.
Bridesmaids	Sisters not chosen to be the maid or matron of honor and female friends and relatives fill these roles.	Modern brides can forgo bridesmaids, if they choose. Or, you can opt to include anyone—male or female— who is special to you.
Best Man	The groom's brother, best friend, or close male relative is the honor attendant on the groom's side.	A brother or relative can still hold this position, but so can a groom's dad or his best female friend—she can be the "best woman." Two brothers or friends can also share the assignment.

	TRADITIONAL	TODAY
Ushers	A certain number of male friends or relatives are chosen to correspond with the number of bridesmaids.	Brides and grooms can make their attendant selections without worrying about having the same number of people on each side. If, for example, there are six bridesmaids and four groomsmen, then two lucky guys can escort a lady on each arm. The only guideline that's still smart to follow: Have at least one usher for every fifty guests—that way you won't end up with a bottleneck of guests waiting to be escorted to their seats for the ceremony.
Flower Girl	Generally, a flower girl is a three- to seven-year-old relative of the bride, such as a niece.	Flower girls can come from the bride or groom's family, or be the child of a close friend. If the bride or groom has a young daughter from a previous relationship, she often fills the role of flower girl.
Ring Bearer	A young boy, usually between three and seven years old, is given the honor of carrying the rings.	Though young boys are still the most common option, some creative couples have given this job to a beloved pet.

Things to Consider When Selecting Your Attendants

- When choosing your bridal party, you and your groom should select the people with whom you are closest. Being a member of the party is an honor you extend to your best buds and favorite family members. That said, you might also consider including a future sister- or brother-in-law or stepchild as a nice gesture—even if you aren't yet that close to them.

- The number of attendants you choose is entirely up to you. If you're having a small, informal affair you may only want one or two attendants. Formal weddings tend to have more attendants—anywhere from five or six to twelve or more. Just keep in mind that the more attendants you have, the bigger chunk of your budget you'll need to earmark for things like flowers and wedding party gifts.

- If you have more special friends and family members than you can include in your bridal party, consider asking them to perform other tasks of honor. For example, they can do readings, sing (assuming, of course, that the person has a good voice), or distribute wedding programs before the ceremony.

- Before you ask people to be part of your bridal party, brush up on what's required of each person. Not sure? See chapter 5: "The Wedding Party" for details about who does what. That way, you'll be prepared in case your chosen pals have any questions about what's expected of them.

- Ask your attendants-to-be well in advance of the wedding. When you ask, be sure to tell them the details you know, especially the wedding date and location (particularly important if you're having a destination wedding). Those you ask needn't answer on the spot. Let them have a few days to decide.

- If someone declines (often due to geography or their financial situation), be gracious. Being a bridesmaid or usher is a significant commitment of time and money so be understanding if someone is unable to take that on. It's not a slight against you, and on the plus side, they're saving you the difficulty of having an attendant who's not fully invested in the wedding.

Can We Talk?

Q: I'm confused. What's the difference between a maid and a matron of honor?

Corinne, 29, New Jersey

A: Those terms confuse many people, but the answer is really quite simple: A maid of honor is the title for an honor attendant who is unmarried. A matron of honor is one who is a Mrs. You can have a maid or a matron of honor—or both. Say, for example, you have two sisters, one who is single and one who is married. Your single sis could be your maid of honor and your married sister your matron. The two would share the duties associated with the bride's honor attendant.

Splitting the Wedding Bills

It used to be that the bride's family footed the bill for the majority of the wedding expenses—from the invitations to the reception to the bride's dress—and the groom's family paid for the rehearsal dinner and little else. See below for a traditional example of how costs are divided.

Traditional Wedding Expense Breakdown

Following are the traditional guidelines regarding who pays for what. You can use these lists as a reference when deciding what division of costs works best for you and your families.

Bride's Family

- Engagement party (optional)
- Wedding invitations and other stationery (announcements, thank-you notes, etc.)
- Services of bridal consultant
- Wedding gown and accessories
- Flowers for ceremony and reception sites
- Bouquets for bridesmaids
- Music
- Photography
- Videography
- Ceremony
- Reception
- Bridal party transportation to ceremony and reception
- Family's wedding attire

Groom's Family

- Engagement party (optional)
- Rehearsal dinner
- Their own wedding attire

The Bride

- The groom's ring
- The bridesmaids' luncheon
- Gifts for the bridesmaids
- Gifts for parents
- Wedding gift for the groom

The Groom

- The bride's rings
- The marriage license
- Officiant's fee
- His formalwear
- Personal flowers: the bride's bouquet, boutonnieres for wedding party, corsages for mothers and grandmothers
- Gifts for the groomsmen
- Wedding gift for the bride
- Gifts for parents
- Honeymoon
- Transportation to the honeymoon

The Wedding Party

- Bridal shower (bridesmaids only)
- Bachelor and bachelorette parties
- Gifts for the couple (can purchase individual gifts or chip in on a group gift)
- Wedding attire and accessories
- Transportation to and from wedding town or city

Today, however, it is less common for the parents of the bride to shoulder the bulk of the financial burden. Instead, many couples are paying for their own weddings or the expenses are being shared by the couple, the bride's parents, and the groom's parents. The parents may offer a set dollar amount for the bride and groom to use as they see fit, or they may each decide to pay for particular items. For example, the bride's family could pay for the ceremony and reception sites, the limousines and the reception food. The groom's family could pay for the rehearsal dinner, all beverages, music, the photographer, and the videographer. And the bride and groom could pay for their wedding attire, flowers, invitations, and wedding cake. Of course, this is just one way to split the costs—you, your groom, and your families will need to work out your own division of costs based on who is able and willing to handle the expenses.

Talking to Your Families About Wedding Costs

Aah, the dreaded money talk. If you're lucky, your families will approach you and your fiancé to let you know what, if anything, they plan to contribute to your wedding. If your parents don't initiate a conversation, you will need to. Yes, broaching the subject of wedding finances can definitely feel awkward, but the sooner you do it, the sooner you can start hammering out a realistic wedding budget.

That said, before you or your fiancé schedule a sit-down with your families, take some time to talk about the type of wedding the two of you envision and figure out what this kind of affair is likely to cost. With that information in mind, it's time to talk to your parents. You and your fiancé can meet with each set of parents together, or you may prefer to speak with your own parents separately. Either way, begin the conversation by explaining the type of wedding you'd like to have and how much money you and your fiancé can afford to spend. Ask your parents if they had planned to help out. Let them know that you are not asking to embarrass them or put them on the spot but just have to determine your overall budget. Thank your parents for any financial assistance they offer, and react graciously if they say they are unable to contribute.

Did You Know?

One common question couples have: Who pays for the bridal party's lodging while they are in town for the wedding? The background: Traditionally, the bride and her family provided a place for the maid of honor and bridesmaids to stay—this could be a private home (possibly the bride's parents' home or the house of a friend or relative in the area) or a hotel, in which case the bride's family would pay for the rooms. The groom and his family usually did the same for his attendants. That practice is less common these days, especially with the increase of destination weddings for which the bride and groom or their families often pick up the cost of their attendants' meals and any planned activities. The bottom line: You don't have to pay for your attendants' lodgings, but it's a nice thing to do if you can swing it.

If your parents are willing to share in the expenses, it's wise to suggest setting up a wedding account in your name and your fiancé's. That way, you can deposit each family's contributions and pay all of the bills from one source. If your families are uncomfortable with that idea and prefer to pay the individual bills for the items they have agreed to provide, that is fine too. Vendors, such as the photographer, can send their bills to you or directly to whomever is paying.

~~ 2 ~~

Pre-Wedding Parties

Fire up that personal digital assistant or have your date book handy—you'll need it to keep track of all the wedding-related events that will be landing on your calendar between now and your actual wedding day! Of course, you'll be penciling in tastings with your wedding cake baker and fittings with your dressmaker, but you'll also enjoy a ton of parties and celebrations such as bridal showers and bachelor and bachelorette parties in your honor. With all the friends and relatives who want to fete you and your future hubby, you'll get a taste of what it's like to be an A-list celebrity with a packed social schedule. Your main jobs as guest of honor at these events: Be gracious, thank everyone for the efforts they're making on your behalf, and, of course, have a blast!

Bridal Shower Basics

Aside from the engagement party, your bridal shower will probably be the first celebratory event during your engagement. Historically, bridal showers were a way for a community to help a bride build a dowry for married life. Today, showers remain a popular way for friends and family to pitch in to outfit a soon-to-be-wed couple's household. What *has* changed is how showers are planned. If the words *bridal shower* make you think of women sipping tea and nibbling on dainty sandwiches, you're only half right! While the traditional bridal shower—a ladies-only luncheon or tea—is still a common choice (and a lovely one at that), it's far from the only option.

Today's bridal showers can take many forms. They can be held in a private home (best for small gatherings) or at a restaurant, club, or other venue. Sit-down or buffet luncheons are still popular, but cocktail parties and informal backyard barbecues are terrific choices as well. The biggest twist: Some brides are forgoing the women-only gathering for a coed, or "Jack and Jill" shower that honors not just you but your beloved too.

If you've been married before, don't feel you have to miss out on the fun of a wedding shower. Having a shower the second time around is perfectly acceptable. However, it may be appropriate for the hosts to keep your guest list intimate and invite only your closest friends and family—that way, they avoid inviting acquaintances who may have "showered" you the first time. Previously married couples or those who have been living together may already have many of the basic household goods they need, so consider a theme shower that would encourage guests to give presents related to the couple's hobbies and interests. But even if couples already have sheets, towels, dishes, and the like, a shower is a great time to upgrade to fresh, new stuff.

The Party Planner

Bridal showers are usually planned and paid for by the maid of honor and the bridesmaids, or by a close friend or relative of the bride or groom who offers to host the get-together. Traditionally, it was considered inappropriate for immediate family—the bride's or groom's mother or sisters, for example – to throw a shower since that could be construed as asking for gifts for the couple. However, it's become more common for a bride's mother or sisters to be involved in shower planning—especially if the sisters are members of the wedding party. In fact, even if the bridesmaids are hosting the shower, it's not unusual for the mother of the bride to contribute to the cost, especially if the party is being held at a restaurant or club. One important point: Whoever is hosting the shower—be it a single person or a group—is responsible for the costs. Guests are never to be asked to contribute to covering the cost of their meal.

Did You Know?

Strictly speaking, etiquette experts say that a bridal shower should take place between two weeks and two months before the wedding. However, many showers are being scheduled earlier—especially if the hosts are trying to surprise the bride.

Guest List Success

Shower invites are usually limited to the people closest to the bride and groom. For a traditional, ladies-only party, the guest list might include mothers, stepmothers, stepdaughters, sisters, aunts, grandmothers, cousins, and close female friends. The mothers of the bride and groom may also have a few close family friends they'd like to include. Who can be left off the list? Believe it or not, some wedding guests. For example, the groom's friends' wives or girlfriends needn't be invited to the shower if they don't know the bride well. Guests who live too far away to make the shower can also be given a pass. Just be sure that everyone invited to the shower is also invited to the wedding. The only exception: office showers thrown by coworkers. In this case, the colleagues who plan and attend a work shower won't necessarily be invited to the wedding.

Inviting Ideas

Shower invitations can be as formal or casual as the host or hosts choose, but like wedding invitations, they should match the style of the event. Most card stores offer a nice selection of premade cards that hosts can fill in with shower details. Other invitation options include ordering printed invites from a stationer or printing them yourself on a computer. The invitations should be in the mail to guests three to four weeks prior to the shower.

To make shopping easier for guests, it is acceptable to include in the invitation the names of the stores where the couple has registered. Some stores even provide printed cards that can be slipped into the invitation envelope. Otherwise, you can simply write, "Sara is registered at [Name of Store]" or "Sara and Tim are registered at [Name of Store]" on the invitation. Once you provide the information, guests can choose to shop from the registry or from another store of their choice.

Sample Bridal Shower Invitations

Shhh! It's a Surprise!

Please join us for a bridal shower honoring

Amanda Reilly

Saturday, April 3, at noon

*The Hunt Club Grille
Sonoma, California*

*Please RSVP by March 15
to Sharon at 212-555-4567*

*The bride-to-be is registered at Fortunoff
1-800-Fortunoff, www.fortunoff.com*

*The Bridal Party [Or, name(s) of
whomever is hosting]*

It's a Bridal Shower!

*Sharon Spector, Natalie Forman, and
Elizabeth Tully*
invite you to join them in showering

Amanda Reilly

with love, best wishes, and household necessities!

*Saturday, April 3, at noon
in the home of Mrs. Anna Reilly
14 Elm Court
Sonoma, California*

RSVP by March 15 to Sharon at 212-555-4567

*The bride-to-be is registered at Fortunoff
1-800-Fortunoff, www.fortunoff.com
Please also bring a small item for the Wishing Well*

Did You Know?

Sometimes shower invitations will indicate that there is a "Wishing Well" for the bride. That means that guests are asked to bring an inexpensive household item (think wooden spoons or a dishtowel) to place in a decorated well-shaped structure (some venues have them on hand; otherwise, they can be rented at most party supply stores). The little goodies for the Wishing Well needn't be gift-wrapped; guests just drop in their offerings.

The Shower Day Game Plan

Generally, showers last between three and four hours—any more than that and guests are likely to get antsy. It's up to the hostess to keep the afternoon or evening moving along smoothly.

If the shower is a surprise, ask guests to arrive half an hour before the bride is expected so they are all there to welcome her and yell "Surprise!" Once the bride makes her grand entrance, she should circulate around the room to greet each of her guests. By the time she's finishing up her hellos, lunch can be served.

After lunch, the bride should take a seat at the front of the room (place a special chair in a spot where all guests will have a good view) and begin opening gifts. Bridesmaids can help the process along by passing the bride her gifts, repacking them, and keeping a record of who gave what (this makes it easy for the bride to send thank-you notes later on). A bridesmaid (pick the craftiest one!) can also be designated to collect the bows and ribbons from the shower gifts and craft them into a "bouquet" (often by attaching them to a paper plate) for the bride to carry at the wedding rehearsal. During this time, dessert, coffee, and tea are served. Once dessert and the gift-opening are completed, guests will begin to say their good-byes.

Sample Thank-You Notes

Even though you'll thank your shower guests in person, it's still nice to send a handwritten note expressing your gratitude after the event. Be sure to mention the gift by name and include a line about how you plan to use it. Here's a basic format you can follow:

Dear Mrs. Jackson,

Thank you very much for the hand mixer. As you know, I love to bake so it will be used often to whip up delicious desserts. I know Bobby will appreciate all of the homemade goodies that I will make! I was so happy that you could attend my shower, and share in the fun.

Fondly,
Allison

Supreme Themes

Plan a shower that will stand out from the crowd with these ideas. Having more than one shower? Hosts can select different themes in order to avoid overlapping presents.

Jack-and-Jill

Bring on the guys! This type of shower gathers together the important men and women in a couple's life to celebrate. The bride and groom are co-guests of honor and share the fun of

Tips for a Successful Shower

- Send out invitations three to four weeks before the shower date.

- If more than one shower is being held, don't invite the same guests to multiple showers. The exception: The bridal party and the bride's and groom's mothers can be invited to each shower (but they don't need to bring a gift each time).

- Bridesmaids should help the bride with her gifts (repacking them carefully so she can move quickly to opening the next) and recording what each guest gave so that the bride has a comprehensive list for writing thank-you notes.

- Showers can be a surprise for the bride, or not. If it won't be a surprise, the bride can offer input for the guest list, but ultimately the budget and number of guests are up to the host.

- If you're the guest of honor at a shower that isn't a surprise, it's polite to give a small gift to your hostess. You can send something in advance of the event—perhaps a pretty flower arrangement that can be used to decorate the buffet table—or bring a small gift with you that day. Also, don't forget to thank your host and follow up with a handwritten thank-you note.

opening the gifts for their new home. When hosting a coed shower, consider choosing a theme like home entertainment or gourmet cooking—guys may be more into opening a DVD player than a place setting of china! Good choices for a Jack-and-Jill shower include a barbecue or lunch or dinner buffet.

Room-by-Room

Make sure the bride gets a variety of gifts to outfit every room in her house by planning a room-by-room shower. How it works:

Can We Talk?

Q: I just found out that my coworkers are planning a bridal shower for me. I hadn't planned on inviting them to my wedding, but should I do so now that I know they're having a shower for me?

Jeanine, 34, Florida

A: Celebrating your upcoming nuptials with an in-office shower is certainly a nice gesture by your colleagues—you're lucky to work with such kind people. Still, if you weren't planning to invite them to your wedding, there is no reason to change your guest list now. Chances are your coworkers just want to help you mark the occasion in some way and don't expect to be invited. So enjoy the shower and know that your only obligation is to be a gracious guest of honor and to thank your coworkers for their generosity.

Assign each guest a specific room of the house to buy for—and mention it in the invitations. Bathroom buyers can give towels, shower curtains, or bath products. Kitchen people can go for baking gear, small appliances, or dishes.

Round-the-Clock

Cover your bride from dawn to dusk with this clever shower idea: Ask each guest to bring a gift that relates to a certain hour of the day. For example, a 7 A.M. guest might give a coffeemaker or waffle iron—perfect for getting the couple's days off to a delicious start. An 11 P.M. guest could wrap up a luxurious sheet set or some sexy lingerie. Have more than twenty-four guests? Double up and designate two or more attendees for each hour of the day.

His-and-Her Hobbies

Whether the engaged couple loves outdoor adventures, traveling, cooking, or gardening, they'll no doubt appreciate a shower tailored to their favorite pastimes. Let your guests know of your plan by sending themed invitations. For instance, mail out flowery invites for a garden shower, or map- or globe-inspired cards for a travel shower. Ask guests to plan their presents accordingly.

Stock-the-Bar

Perfect for a couple who loves to entertain, a stock-the-bar shower gets them set up for lots of future gatherings of friends and family. Guests shower the couple with gifts like wine, glasses, and cocktail shakers. Try this idea for a coed shower, since the gift options are so guy-friendly. Get the word out with invitations made to look like wine bottles.

Around-the-World

Take the bride or couple on a trip around the world—without leaving the room. Send out invitations with a travel theme—an airline boarding pass invitation is one idea—and ask guests to bring gifts associated with a certain country. Gifts representing France can include a cheese board and knife or champagne glasses and a bottle of bubbly; China can mean a wok and chopsticks; and Italy-inspired guests can contribute a pasta maker, wineglasses, or a pizza-making set.

The Bridesmaids' Luncheon

Some brides choose to host a special bridesmaids' luncheon to thank their attendants for their help and support throughout the wedding-planning process. This event, which is usually scheduled for a few weeks before the wedding, can take place at a restaurant or at the bride's home. The guest list: you, your maid or matron of honor, and your bridesmaids. If your bridesmaids won't be gathered in one location until just days before the wedding, you can hold the bridesmaids' luncheon then. Another option: Since the days leading up to the wedding can be very hectic and may not allow for another party, treat your 'maids to lunch, dinner, or drinks on the day you shop for their dresses.

If you do have a bridesmaids' luncheon, consider incorporating the traditional charm cake into your celebration—chances are it will spark some great conversations. How it works: You purchase a set of charms that are baked into a cake with each charm's ribbon "handle" left showing. Before the cake is cut for dessert, each bridesmaid pulls a ribbon to retrieve a charm. Different charms have different meanings. A horseshoe, for example, signifies good luck and a ring means that woman will be the next to marry.

The bridesmaids' luncheon is also a good time to distribute the gifts you purchased for your bridesmaids. (See chapter 4: "The Rehearsal Dinner" for great gift ideas.) Alternatively, you can hand out your bridesmaids' presents at the rehearsal dinner.

The Bachelor Party

Do the words *bachelor party* instantly bring to mind bars, booze, and half-naked babes jumping out of cakes? Well, the definition of this traditional male ritual has changed for many modern men. Historically, guys bid adieu to their single days with one last night of hard-core carousing—often involving copious amounts of alcohol and a visit to a strip club. While that's not completely unheard of these days, many guys are opting for tamer pursuits. Some common guy get-togethers: a golf outing or softball game followed by dinner and drinks, a weekend camping getaway, or a trip to a casino.

A bachelor party, usually planned and hosted by the best man, can technically be scheduled any time, but it's best to do it several weeks before the wedding. Definitely steer clear of the night before the wedding because a hungover groom or groomsman is never a good thing! As far as paying, each guest should cover his own evening's entertainment, and many groups pitch in to pay for the groom's night out.

Can We Talk?

Q: I trust my fiancé, but I'm still a little concerned about the crazy things he and his buddies might do at his bachelor party. How should I handle my fears?

Angela, 25, Arizona

A: First, know that you aren't alone. The thought of a bachelor party makes many a bride-to-be a little nervous. Your best bet: Talk to your groom and share your concerns. Chances are he just wants to blow off some steam with his pals in a harmless way. While it's unfair to expect your guy to forgo this tradition, good communication between the two of you can help ensure that you both get through the night unscathed.

The Bachelorette Party

Why should the guys have all the fun? Many brides and their pals choose to celebrate the bride's last days as a single woman with a girls' night out (or in!). While drinking and male revues are still on the agenda for some women (Chippendale's, anyone?), women are taking advantage of some alternatives to barhopping. They are pampering themselves with spa visits, meeting up for a night of cooking lessons or craft-making, or gathering for an evening at a tea house or swank lounge where they can sip sophisticated cocktails and bond with their buds.

Bachelorette blowouts are most often organized by the maid of honor and/or bridesmaids, and can be scheduled for the same night as the bachelor party. Guests—typically the bridesmaids and the bride's closest friends—usually pay their own way and often choose to chip in to treat the bride.

Bright Idea

Want to combine your options? Plan separate bachelor/bachelorette gatherings—say a spa visit for the gals, a golf outing for the guys—then arrange for everyone to meet for dinner or drinks at a popular nightspot.

Joint Bachelor/Bachelorette Party

A third type of party that's been gaining popularity with some couples is the combo bachelor-bachelorette bash. Instead of heading off in separate directions, brides and grooms are gathering their friends in one location and combining their so-long-to-single-days celebrations. These doubleheaders are great for brides and grooms who share many mutual friends, or for couples who want to introduce friends from different times in their lives, from high school to college to the working world. What to do? Dinner and drinks are a classic combo. But activities such as linedancing or a visit to a comedy club are fun options too.

3

Invitations and Wedding Announcements

Between all the bills and junk mail that fill our mailboxes these days, it's not often we actually *want* to open the envelopes addressed to us. The exception: a beautiful wedding invitation. The weight of the paper, the elegant calligraphy on the envelope, and the carefully chosen "Love" postage stamps make receiving an invitation a treat for your guests. Besides telling them the whens and wheres of your wedding celebration, the invitation gives your friends and relatives their first hint of the tone and style of your affair. As the saying goes, you don't get a second chance to make a first impression, so take the time to find an invitation that conveys just the right feeling.

Choosing Your Invitation

Bows, and overlays, and colored ink—oh my! As you'll quickly find out, there are tons of options when it comes to wedding invitations. The only "rule" you need to follow: Pick an invitation that matches the style of your wedding. For example, an invitation with a shell motif will set the tone for a romantic seaside ceremony while a formally worded ivory card with black ink will let them know to expect a sophisticated city soiree. Finding the right invitation can take time, so start early—six to eight months before your date should give you plenty of time to request and review sample invites and allow for your chosen ones to be printed. Even if you want to create your own invitations, allow yourself several months, since the process can be time-consuming. Finally, if you're having an intimate wedding with a guest list of fewer than fifty, you might consider using handwritten notes to notify your guests. Not many people send handwritten invitations, so yours would be sure to get a lot of attention.

Printing Options

We've all heard the saying "What are you waiting for—an engraved invitation?" but most of us don't know exactly what an engraved invitation is! So here's the scoop: Traditional engraving is an intensive process in which letters are pressed into the paper (if you turn the paper over, you can feel them). The downside: Engraving is very costly. Since it's so expensive, many couples today opt for an alternative printing process called thermography, which creates a raised print that isn't etched into the paper. It looks virtually identical but can cost as much as 50 percent less.

If you are printing your own invites on your home computer, a laser printer will provide the most professional-looking results. Surf the Web to find a variety of fonts—you're sure to hit on one that's right for your invitation. Neatness counts, so be sure to use a font that fits the style of your wedding (formal vs. casual) and feed your invitations into the printer carefully so that the result is straight and lined up correctly. A smeared or crooked invitation is definitely *not* the first thing you want your guests to see!

What to Include in Your Invitation

Not every family fits the two-married-parents-living-in-the-same-house mold. For that reason, there are as many variations on invitation wording as there are family situations. The common thread in all wedding invitations is that they must indicate the following information:

- Who is hosting the wedding
- Time
- Date
- Location of the ceremony
- Level of formality
- Location of the wedding reception (unless you're using a separate reception card)
- Any special information, such as whether the reception will offer only cake and champagne in lieu of a full meal, or the wedding is outdoors so guests can dress accordingly.

Did You Know?

It is only considered correct to use the phrase "request the honour of your presence" on your invitation if your ceremony is taking place in a house of worship such as a church or synagogue. If you're exchanging vows at a country club, restaurant, hotel, or other venue, use the phrase "request the pleasure of your company" instead.

Here's a look at the traditional wording of a wedding invitation:

Mr. and Mrs. Matthew James Hayden
request the honour of your presence
at the marriage of their daughter
Victoria Lynn
to
Kyle William Banks
Saturday, the ninth of September
Two thousand and six
at half after three o'clock
St. Thomas Church
Springfield, Massachusetts
Reception immediately following
Glen Brook Country Club

OR

Mr. and Mrs. Matthew James Hayden

request the honour of your presence

at the marriage of their daughter

Victoria Lynn

to

Kyle William Banks

son of

Mr. and Mrs. William Stanley Banks

Saturday, the ninth of September

Two thousand and six

at half after three o'clock

St. Thomas Church

Springfield, Massachusetts

Reception immediately following

Glen Brook Country Club

If your reception is not immediately following the ceremony, or if some are not invited to both the ceremony and the reception, leave off the last two lines above and instead include a printed reception card—more about those later—with the invitation.

Depending on your personal circumstances, you may need to modify the above wording a bit. How? See Appendix A for examples for divorced or deceased parents, co-hosts, military couples, and more.

Wording Do's and Don'ts

Attention to detail is crucial when it comes to creating an invitation that you can be proud of. Keep these tips in mind when ordering or making your invitations.

Do spell out times, as in six o'clock, instead of using abbreviations, such as 6 P.M.

Don't use nicknames or shorthand versions of titles. For example, write Doctor Ann Walsh instead of Dr. Ann Walsh, and Alexander Stanford, Junior, instead of Alex Stanford, Jr.

Do use the British spellings of words such as honour and favour.

Don't use punctuation marks except for commas after the day of the week and between city and state names.

Do spell out all words, including those that are commonly abbreviated such as "Street," "Avenue," or "Boulevard."

Don't leave your invitees guessing. Clue them in to what to expect with indicators such as "Black tie" on the reception invitation.

Invitation Enclosures

Pop quiz: What's the difference between a response card and an admission card? No clue? That's okay. We'll explain in our quick crash course on wedding enclosures—a.k.a. all those printed items that you'll carefully tuck into the envelope with your wedding invitation. Here's a look at what each piece is for, as well as when and how they should be used. Hint: You'll need some, but probably not all, for your wedding.

The Reception Card

If you are inviting each guest to both your wedding ceremony and reception, and if the reception immediately follows your "I do's," then you can print the party information right on the actual invitation card. If not, you'll need to include a separate item, called a reception card, that outlines the time and place of your reception. This information should be printed on a card that is similar to, but smaller than, your actual invitation. Below are a few acceptable ways to word your reception card.

This wording works well when you are inviting guests only to the reception and not the ceremony. When might that be the case? If you choose to have a private ceremony but a large reception.

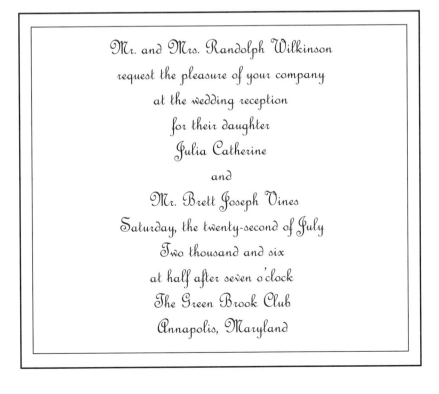

Mr. and Mrs. Randolph Wilkinson
request the pleasure of your company
at the wedding reception
for their daughter
Julia Catherine
and
Mr. Brett Joseph Vines
Saturday, the twenty-second of July
Two thousand and six
at half after seven o'clock
The Green Brook Club
Annapolis, Maryland

This wording can be used for your reception card when your ceremony and reception are taking place at two different locations.

> *Reception immediately following the ceremony*
> *The Green Brook Club*
> *Annapolis, Maryland*

You can use this set-up to inform guests of both the time and location of your fete.

> *Reception*
> *at half after seven o'clock*
> *The Green Brook Club*
> *Annapolis, Maryland*

The Response Card

Years ago, printed response cards—which are used regularly today—didn't exist. Guests knew to respond to a formal invitation with a handwritten note on their own stationery. However, since that tradition has faded with time, most of today's brides and grooms include a printed response card with their invitation. The response card can simply be a coordinating piece of stationery with blank space for guests to write in their reply and a line that reads, "The favour of a reply is requested." Though technically not necessary, many couples include a reply date (as in "The favour of your reply is requested by the first of June") to increase the likelihood of receiving timely responses. Alternately, a response card can be worded like this:

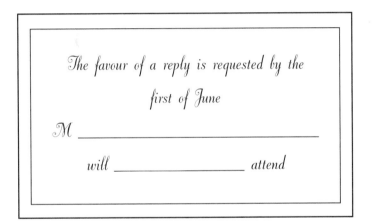

The favour of a reply is requested by the

first of June

M _____

will _____ *attend*

In this case, the "M" line is where the guest can enter his or her name. For example, Miss or Ms. Kelly Rutherford or Mr. and Mrs. Samuel Johnson. After that, they can fill in a "gladly" if they can make it or "not" if they can't.

When using a response card, be sure to provide each guest with a stamped addressed envelope so they can easily return their reply. The return envelope is usually addressed to whomever is hosting the wedding.

Maps and Directions

With many friends and family living out of town and even out of state, a map and directions are a key part of the wedding invitation. After all, a guest can't help you celebrate your day if he or she can't find the place! There are a few things to keep in mind when creating these aids.

- Be absolutely certain that the directions are correct by driving the route yourself. It sounds obvious, but often couples rely on Internet direction websites, which are great—but not always correct. Double check the route and you won't have to worry about Great Aunt Martha getting lost on the way to the church.

- Make sure the presentation of the map and directions is neat and easy to read. Photocopies (which are often provided by catering facilities and houses of worship) are okay as long as they don't look like your four-year-old niece was running the copier. Smudges, crooked lines, and words running off the page are all no-no's. Directions and maps can also be printed on card stock that coordinates with your invitation and other stationery materials.

- If you're following the strictest protocol, you should send the map and directions in a separate mailing once the guest has accepted your invitation. These days, though, it's more efficient, cost effective, and perfectly acceptable to include the directions with your invitation.

Hotel Information

For friends and family coming in from out of town and local guests who don't want to worry about driving home after a night of partying, it's a thoughtful gesture to include information about accommodations close to your wedding location. If possible, try to reserve a block of rooms for your guests and negotiate a group rate. It's also nice to include a few hotel options that are in different price ranges so guests can find something they'll be comfortable with. (Some will just want a clean place to sleep without spending a lot of money, while others might prefer to splurge on a hotel with more amenities.) Then you can simply inform everyone of the arrangements via an insert card with the invitation, or you can send it along earlier with your save-the-date card.

The Rain Card

They say rain on your wedding day is good luck. Still, it's best not to test fate when planning an outdoor wedding. Always have a backup plan! The best way to inform guests of your "Plan B" is to include a rain card with your invitation. How it works: The rain card can be worded in this manner: "In case of rain, the ceremony and reception will take place at LeGrande Park Atrium." That way, wet guests won't be wandering around trying to locate your alternate spot.

Less common these days, but still used on occasion and included with the wedding invitation are:

The Admission Card. Unless you're a celebrity or you're getting married in an extraordinary location—a landmark church that attracts scores of tourists, for example—you won't need an admission card. But if your location requires them, admission cards should be included with a guest's invitation.

The "Within the Ribbon" Card. Also known as "pew cards," within the ribbon cards are given to special guests. When the guest arrives at the ceremony, she shows her card to the usher escorting her so he knows that she should get a prime seat (often in a section of pews marked with ribbons).

At Home Cards. An old-fashioned staple, at home cards tell guests when and where the new Mr. and Mrs. will be starting their life together. They often look like this:

At home

after May fifteenth

125 Main Street

Baltimore, Maryland 21210

(410) 555-1234

Envelope Etiquette

What goes on the outer envelope—the one that is stamped and addressed? What goes on the inner? Even something as seemingly simple as a mailing envelope can be tricky when it comes to your wedding invitations. To get yours right, keep these guidelines in mind.

- The correct way to address the outer envelope to a married couple is: *Mr. and Mrs. Marcus Fine.* The corresponding inner envelope should say: *Mr. and Mrs. Fine.*

- If one spouse is a doctor, you can address the outer envelope to *Doctor and Mrs. William Randall,* or to *Doctor Renee Mackenzie* and *Mr. Scott Meyers* (in the latter case, the names would go on separate lines). The inside envelopes should read *Doctor and Mrs. Randall,* or *Doctor Mackenzie and Mr. Meyers.*

- When addressing an envelope (outer or inner) to two doctors, the correct format is *The Doctors Egan*.

- If you are inviting a married couple and their children, then write: *Mr. and Mrs. Marcus Fine* on the outer envelope and on the inner envelope write *Mr. and Mrs. Fine* (on the first line) and *Ryan, Kaitlynn, and Colleen* (on the second line).

Assembling Your Invitation

It may seem like putting your invitation mailings together requires the dexterity of an origami master, but it's actually quite simple. Place the invitation itself and the related materials (reception cards, response cards, and so on) in the inner envelope—which will remain unsealed—in this order:

1. Main invitation (position so the text facing is up)

2. Tissue paper (historically used to prevent the ink on the invitation from smearing; serves no practical purpose today so you can skip it if you want)

3. Reception card (if you are using one)

4. All other cards in size order with the smallest on top (this would include the response card—which should be tucked under the flap of the response envelope—maps, directions, pew cards, etc.)

If you are using a folded invitation, all of the above items (except the tissue) should go between the folds.

Insert the inner envelope into the outer envelope so that the guest's name is facing the flap of the outer envelope and is what you see when the outer envelope is opened. Whew! You're finished!

- Guests over age eighteen who live with their parents should receive their own invitations, rather than be grouped with their parents.

¥When sending an invitation to an unmarried couple who lives together, put the names on separate lines in alphabetical order. The same goes for married couples who have different last names. For example, the outer envelope should say:

Ms. Dana Kendall
Mr. Nicholas Simon

- The corresponding inner envelope should say:

Ms. Kendall and Mr. Simon

- Unmarried couples who don't live together should each receive an invitation at their own homes.

- Never address the outer envelope "and Guest." If you don't know the name of someone's significant other, say the husband of a coworker, ask the person you do know for the other's name. If a friend or relative is invited with a guest but doesn't have a significant other, address the outer envelope to your friend or relative and then write "and Guest" on the inner envelope only.

¥Have the envelopes (both inner and outer) hand-addressed by a calligrapher or someone with attractive handwriting. Or, print the envelopes on a home computer using a nice font and black ink.

Can We Talk?

Q: I'm having a formal, adults-only reception. How can I politely let my guests know that children aren't invited?

Aimee, 25, New York

A: The way you address the invitation envelopes tells guests specifically who is invited to the event. If you address the outer envelope to Mr. and Mrs. Sean Morgan and the inner envelope to Mr. and Mrs. Morgan, this tells guests that only those two people are invited. If you are concerned about hurt feelings, you might consider enclosing a handwritten note to those with children explaining that as much as you would love to invite their children, you are simply unable to do so. You can also mention (if it's true!) that their children are welcome to attend the ceremony. Finally, if a guest calls and asks you if she can bring her children, simply (and kindly) say you are afraid not. And don't worry: You're not making an etiquette misstep by saying "no," she's making one by asking.

Bright Idea

If you're crunched for time, ask the printer to send the envelopes ahead of the rest of your order. That way you can get a jump on addressing them while the invitations themselves are being printed.

Invitation Countdown

Not sure when to call in the calligrapher and when to head to the post office? Follow this countdown to get your invites in the mail on time.

Six to Eight Months Before the Wedding

- Start looking for invitations.

- Request samples of your favorites.

- Begin working on your invitations if you are making them yourself.

Four to Five Months Before the Wedding

- Gather information for maps or directions. Take a test run rather than rely on your memory or online direction programs.

- Choose a response date. It should usually be three to four weeks before your wedding, and at least in time to give your caterer a final head count (usually several days to one week before your wedding).

- Order your invitations, enclosures, and other stationery needs such as thank-you notes. Be sure to order twenty or so extra to cover last-minute additions to the guest list and to save as mementos. Extra envelopes are a must for misspellings and errors.

- Hire a calligrapher, or leave yourself (or a willing pal with nice handwriting) enough time to address the inner and outer envelopes.

Ten to Twelve Weeks Before the Wedding

- Assemble a complete invitation and bring it to the post office to be weighed.

- Buy postage. Don't forget stamps for the response card envelopes.

- Finish assembling the invitations. To make this task go quickly, invite your bridesmaids or friends over to help you stuff envelopes.

Eight to Ten Weeks Before the Wedding
- Mail your A-list invitations.

Six to Eight Weeks Before the Wedding
- If you're using a B-list, mail those invites no later than six weeks before the wedding.

Three to Four Weeks Before the Wedding
- Make follow-up phone calls to any guests who haven't responded. Consider recruiting your mom and mother-in-law to call their MIA guests.

- Give your caterer the final guest count.

- Start working on seating arrangements.

Can We Talk?

Q: I did not get an RSVP from one of my guests and when I called to follow up, the person still wouldn't commit! What should I do?

Christine, 29, Connecticut

A: Assume the person is not coming. If he or she calls to accept later on, it's okay to say, "I'm sorry, but since we didn't hear from you, we assumed you weren't able to attend. It's too late to tell the caterer otherwise."

Who Makes the Cut?

One of the biggest decisions you and your fiancé will face is whom to invite to your wedding. Certain family members and close friends are a given, but unless you have an enormous venue and a sky's-the-limit budget, you'll need to make some tough calls about relatives, coworkers, acquaintances, and the like to keep your guest list in check. But don't panic! There are ways to maintain your sanity—and keep your friends happy—while trimming your guest list.

The first step: Look at your wedding budget and decide how many people you can afford to host. Once you've got a number in mind, it's time to divide that total among yourself, your fiancé, your parents, and your future in-laws. This can get tricky. A fair way to do it: Allot each family the same number of spots on the guest list or divide the list in thirds with you and your fiancé and each set of parents getting a third. Also, keep in mind that often the person who is covering the cost of the wedding gets more say in how the invitations are divided.

Some common guest-list questions have to do with whether to include children, coworkers, and the infamous "and Guest." Here, the etiquette on handling these potentially sticky situations.

Kids or No Kids?

Whether or not to invite children to participate in your wedding celebration is a completely personal decision (though friends and family may be more than willing to offer their input!). Some couples love the idea of including little ones in their special day; others prefer to make it a grown-up affair. Whatever you decide, it's best to make a "rule" (for instance, no children under thirteen years old) and stick with it—any exceptions are bound to cause hurt feelings. If you or your fiancé have children, you'll certainly want to include them in your wedding day—but including your own kids doesn't require you to invite other children as well.

9-to-5 Friends

You no doubt spend a lot of time with your coworkers, but that doesn't necessarily mean they all rate an invitation to your wedding. However, following a few rules will ensure you don't make a faux pas that could land you in hot water at the office. If you are going to invite anyone from the office, you should extend an invitation to your boss out of respect. If you have an assistant, it's also a nice gesture to invite him or her. If your department or office consists of just a few people (say four or five) it's best to go the all-or-none route so you don't step on any toes. And keep in mind that when you invite coworkers you should also invite their significant others (though you aren't required to invite single coworkers with guests). Once you've issued your invitations, ask your work friends to be discreet and force yourself (we know it's hard!!) to keep the wedding chatter to a minimum.

The Great Date Debate

Whether or not to invite family and friends to their wedding with a date is a common quandary for brides and grooms—and you're

Did You Know?

Typically, between 25 and 30 percent of a couple's guests decline their invitation. Still, resist the temptation to overinvite on the assumption that a quarter of the people will say no. Otherwise, you risk ending up with more guests than you can handle!

likely to hear different "rules" about what is proper. Your cousin may swear that anyone over age eighteen must be invited with a date, while your best friend tells you that no one is guaranteed a spot for their partner. Who's right? Well, neither. The real answer: Include the significant others of invited guests, but you don't have to invite single, unattached people with dates (though it's a gracious gesture if you do). What separates the "significant others" from the casual daters? If an invited guest is married, engaged, living with someone, or in a relationship of six months or more, it is appropriate to invite the partner.

A-List and B-List Etiquette

Having trouble keeping your guest list within reasonable boundaries? One way to include as many people as possible without overextending yourself is to create an A-list and a B-list. The A-list invites go out first, and then as those guests decline, you can send out a corresponding number of B-list invitations.

The A-list would consist of those people who you simply couldn't imagine not having at your wedding: your immediate family, grandparents, closest friends, and other VIPs in your life. The B-list could include old school friends that you keep in touch with from time to time, colleagues of your parents, coworkers, and others who would be "nice to have" if possible. Can't decide if someone belongs on the A-list or the B-list? Ask yourself whether that person will likely still be in your life in three to five years. If the answer is yes, add her to the A-list. If not, put her on the B-list.

One caveat about A-list/B-list arrangements: Finding out that you're a guest on the B-list is kind of like finding out you were only hired for your job because your boss's first-choice candidate turned it down—not a nice feeling. So to save on hurt egos, you need to be savvy about how you send off your invitations. Two things to keep in mind: One, don't indicate in any way that there is an A-list and a B-list (a notation on the invitation or envelope, for example, or by sending best friends invitations at different times; if they compare notes, they'll know the later recipient was on the B-list). Two, send out your A-list invitations eight to ten weeks before your wedding and have the B-list invitations ready to mail, as needed. That way, you won't be sending out any B-list invitations suspiciously late in the game.

Advance Notice: Sending Save-the-Date Cards

Your invitation may be the first formal information your guests receive about your nuptial plans; however, in certain situations it's smart to preface the actual invite with a save-the-date card—a casual "heads-up" about the date and location of your wedding. Though not required, these missives can be a lifesaver since they give guests extra notice and can ensure that you get a better turnout for your big event. Think about using a save-the-date card when:

- **Your wedding is scheduled for a holiday weekend.** People's date books tend to fill up quickly for these days. You'll increase the odds of guests sharing your big day if you alert them to your wedding date before they plan their Memorial Day beach weekend or holiday cruise to the Caribbean.

- **Your wedding will take place in a location that gets very busy during certain times of the year.** Seasonal spots like beach-front properties or hotels near ski resorts book up early, so your guests will need extra notice if they want to book a room.

- **Many of your guests will have to travel for the wedding.** Traveling takes time and planning, so let your guests know your date and location well in advance. That way, they can take vacation from work, if needed, and make arrangements for transportation and accommodations.

Bright Idea

Save-the-date cards are usually mailed out six to eight months before you tie the knot, but they can be sent just as soon as you've confirmed your wedding date and determined your guest list. Get them out early—that's one more thing you can check off your wedding to-do list!

The format you choose for your save-the-date cards is entirely up to you. But since these notes are less formal than the actual invitation, why not have a little fun with them? To liven them up, take into account the season or location of your wedding. Hosting a fall fete? Select a card with pretty foliage or rich autumn colors. If you have already chosen your wedding colors, send save-the-date cards in those hues. For a small wedding, send handwritten postcards. For a bigger celebration, print cards on your computer or splurge on professionally printed cards. When it comes to wording, you can be plain and simple:

Save the Date!
Maureen and Anthony
are getting married!
March 23, 2006
Boston, Massachusetts
Formal invitation to follow

OR:

Save the Date
for the wedding of
Mary Marks
and
Adam Goldman
April 10, 2007
Manassas, Virginia
Formal invitation to follow

Or lighthearted:

He asked.
She said "yes!"
Anne and Alex
are tying the knot!
July 24, 2005
Farmington, Pennsylvania
Formal invitation to follow

Wedding Announcements

Wedding announcements, which should be mailed the day after your wedding, do just what the name implies: They announce to the world that you've become Mr. and Mrs.

Who should get these printed notes? Only people who weren't invited to the wedding.

You can mail them off to people like business associates and acquaintances with whom you'd like to share the news of your marriage. Another time wedding announcements are used: if a couple elopes or has a small wedding away from home with few or no guests in attendance. It's best to mail wedding announcements the day after you exchange vows, but up to several months afterward is acceptable.

Like wedding invitations, announcements can come from the couple, the bride's parents, or both sets of parents. Here is the correct wording for each situation:

Mr. and Mrs. Joseph Anderson

have the honour of announcing

the marriage of their daughter

Katherine Michelle

to

Mr. Zachary Sinclair

Sunday, the twenty-seventh of November

Two thousand and five

Sonoma, California

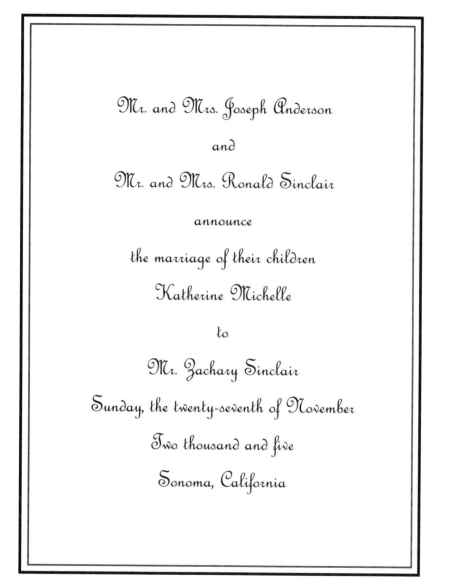

Mr. and Mrs. Joseph Anderson

and

Mr. and Mrs. Ronald Sinclair

announce

the marriage of their children

Katherine Michelle

to

Mr. Zachary Sinclair

Sunday, the twenty-seventh of November

Two thousand and five

Sonoma, California

Katherine Michelle Anderson

and

Zachary Sinclair

announce with pleasure

their marriage

Sunday, the twenty-seventh of November

Two thousand and five

Sonoma, California

Did You Know?

Wedding announcements are intended to share your good news with friends and relatives who weren't invited to the wedding. Those who receive them are not obligated to send a gift.

4

The Rehearsal Dinner

The wedding is almost here! Which means it's time for the rehearsal and the rehearsal dinner. Like a theater rehearsal, your wedding run-though will give you and everyone else involved in your ceremony the chance to practice how to walk, where to stand, and how to recognize the myriad other "cues" they'll need to know to play their role flawlessly. After all, your wedding is a once-in-a-lifetime production and no cast can be expected to perform well without some practice! Once everyone feels satisfied that they know what to do, it's off to the rehearsal dinner—typically a laid-back event involving lots of introductions (don't forget that not everyone in your wedding knows each other), sentimental and humorous toasts, and heartfelt thank-you speeches from you and your groom to your families and friends.

Places, Everyone

The evening begins with the rehearsal, which takes place at your ceremony location. Typically, the officiant explains what everyone's responsibilities will be on the wedding day, and guides the bride and groom, parents, and bridal party through the basics of the ceremony so everyone is comfortable with their entrances, exits, and everything that happens in between. (Don't forget to bring the "bow bouquet" from your bridal shower to hold as you practice walking down the aisle!)

Did You Know?

In some situations—such as when your wedding involves a small number of people or consists of a very simple ceremony—a rehearsal may not be necessary. Instead, your officiant may meet with the ceremony participants briefly on the morning of the wedding. Even so, you can still have a rehearsal dinner. After all, that's when everyone involved in the wedding gathers together, and the fun really begins.

After the rehearsal is wrapped up, the rehearsal dinner begins. Since the rehearsal dinner is typically smaller and more casual than the wedding reception, it affords you an opportunity to relax and bond with your friends and family. Enjoy every minute of it because your actual wedding day will likely fly by without you spending much one-on-one time with your guests. To make the rehearsal dinner pleasant for everyone, be sure to introduce guests to one another so everyone feels at ease and is included in the festivities.

Timing It Right

Most couples hold their rehearsal dinner the night before the wedding, but some do it a day or two in advance since things can get really hectic at the last minute. If your bridal party will be in the area a few days before the wedding, a Thursday night rehearsal dinner can work well for a Saturday wedding. Before you book a venue, check with your officiant to be sure that he or she is available and that your house of worship or other ceremony site isn't booked for another event.

Picking Up the Tab

Planning and paying for the rehearsal dinner was traditionally the groom's parents' responsibility. Some still choose to follow

Can We Talk?

Q: My fiancé's parents are divorced. Should we expect his mother, father, or both to host the rehearsal dinner?

Jamie, 28, Oregon

A: If your fiancé's parents have an amicable relationship, they might choose to co-host the dinner and each contribute to the cost. Your fiancé might remind them that if they decide to co-host, it doesn't mean they will have to act like a couple and spend the entire evening at each other's side. Rather, they would be participating in the festivities because of the role they have in common—parent to your fiancé. If splitting the bill and the co-hosting duties isn't a feasible solution, your fiancé should approach the parent who has the better financial situation to find out if that person is willing to pay for the dinner. If both of your fiancé's parents are unwilling or unable to handle the expense, then you and your fiancé can pay for the evening and allow his parents to "host," if you feel comfortable with that.

that tradition, but it's also perfectly fine for the couple, the bride's parents, or anyone else who offers to host, to cover expenses.

Making the Guest List

Unlike the wedding itself, deciding who to invite to the rehearsal dinner is pretty simple. You must include all members of the bridal party (plus their spouses or dates); parents of the flower girls or ring bearers (if you are inviting the children themselves); both sets of parents; stepparents; grandparents; siblings (and their spouses or significant others); and the officiant and his or her spouse or partner. It's also nice to invite any out-of-town guests who have arrived for the wedding, or to invite all of your guests if your wedding is a destination affair. However, if you'd rather keep your rehearsal dinner more intimate, you can schedule a separate event (cocktails and/or dinner at a restaurant, the hotel where they're staying, or a friend's house) for those guests not directly involved in the ceremony rehearsal.

Issuing Invitations

Since the rehearsal dinner is its own event, it warrants its own set of invitations. You can invite your guests via phone calls if you have a super-small group or send out written invitations for a larger gathering. There's no need to splurge on printed invitations, unless that is important to you; you can pick up preprinted cards at your card or stationery store and simply fill in the details. Hold off on sending rehearsal dinner invitations until after you've received the wedding responses (you don't want to invite someone to the rehearsal dinner who isn't able to make the wedding). Finally, include an RSVP phone number or e-mail address on your invitations. Even if your bash is very informal, you'll need an accurate head count to plan the meal.

Rehearsal Dinner Ideas

The only real "rule" when it comes to planning a rehearsal dinner: Don't plan an event more elaborate than the wedding reception. Consider these options:

- Dinner in a private room at a favorite restaurant (maybe even the place you and your fiancé had your first date)
- A dinner cruise on a local river or lake
- A catered meal that corresponds with your honeymoon destination (try paella if you're Barcelona-bound or French fare if you'll be jetting off to Paris)
- Pizza parlor
- Hibachi restaurant where guests are seated around the grill
- Take-out Mexican or Chinese food at your home (or your parents' home)
- Picnic in the park

Treasured Traditions

Though rehearsal dinners are typically laid-back occasions, there are a few special traditions that most include. One of these is a series of toasts by the host (who's footing the bill), best man, and others. It's customary for toasts to happen in this order:

1. *The host of the evening, often the father of the groom*

2. *The best man*

3. *Groom to bride and her family*

4. *Bride to groom and his family*

5. *Other guests who wish to say a few words*

Since it's a more intimate gathering, the toasts given at the rehearsal dinner can be a little longer and more lighthearted than those given at the wedding. When you and your fiancé take your turns to speak (if you choose to do so), it's a nice gesture to say some kind words about your future spouse as well as to thank both sets of parents. Finally, your fiancé can tie up the speaking portion of the evening with a few last words to the group.

Another rehearsal dinner tradition is for the bride and groom to hand out the gifts they have selected for their wedding party and for their parents. (You and your fiancé can also exchange gifts with each other, if you choose.)

Finally, since one element of the rehearsal dinner is celebrating the lives of the bride and groom, some family members or friends plan brief video or photo presentations featuring special moments from the couple's pasts.

Did You Know?

If you're the one being toasted (for example, when you're the bride and the best man is toasting you and your new hubby), stay seated and don't pick up your glass or sip from it. Simply smile and say thank you when your toaster has finished.

How to Give a Great Toast

Nervous about taking the mike? Don't be. With these tips, you'll be toasting like a seasoned professional.

- **Be sure everyone has something to toast with.** Before you begin your toast, check that everyone's glass is filled.

- **Stand and raise your glass.** When giving a toast, you should rise and hold out your glass.

- **Keep it short and sweet.** People tend to have short attention spans and will appreciate a concise tribute. Keep your toast to no more than three or four minutes, tops.

- **Write it down.** Avoid rambling by writing out your speech on a note card, or at least jotting down a few key ideas. Try not to read it word for word, though. At least look up a few times and make eye contact with those around you.

- **Share a story—but not an embarrassing one.** The point of a toast is to honor the toastee, not embarrass him or her. Offer a sweet or sentimental anecdote but don't say anything vulgar or upsetting.

- **Avoid inside jokes.** Inside jokes just make those on the outs feel uncomfortable. It's a quick way to put a damper on any gathering.

- **Use humor sparingly.** If you have a funny line or two it's fine to include it, but now's not the time to act like you're auditioning for a comedy club.

- **Practice.** Run through your toast a few times beforehand, and you'll feel more confident for the real thing.

- **Don't drink too much.** Having a few drinks to "loosen up" may seem like a good idea at the time. But anyone who's witnessed a drunken, incoherent toast can tell you it's not a wise move.

Bridal Party Gift Ideas

Show your 'maids and men how much you appreciate their support and effort by gifting them with a present you know they will love. The key isn't how much money you spend, but how much thought you put into selecting it. Still, your attendant gift isn't a place to cut corners. After all, these folks have likely spent a considerable amount of time and money to be part of your wedding party. Some couples choose to give each of their attendants a different gift based on that person's hobbies or interests. Others give all the women the same thing and all the men the same thing. Still others give a uniform gift to the bridesmaids and groomsmen but single out the maid of honor and best man for more elaborate gifts. It's your call. Don't forget to enclose a personal note (or an individual poem, if you're word-savvy) with each gift. Some suggestions:

For the Bridesmaids

- Jewelry—choose a pretty necklace, bracelet, or earrings that she can wear on the day of the wedding and beyond

- Gift certificate for a spa treatment

- Silk pajamas

- Personalized stationery with each woman's name or monogram

- Picture frame with a picture of you and your pal

- Engraved jewelry box

- Silk or cashmere wrap

For the Groomsmen

- Engraved flasks or beer mugs

- Tickets to a sporting event

- Monogrammed business card holder

- Cigars with cigar cutter or humidor
- Cuff links
- Monogrammed money clip or pen set
- Pocket knives/tools

For the Flower Girl

- Necklace or earrings
- Monogrammed picture frame
- Jewelry box
- Little girl's purse

For the Ring Bearer

- Silver bank
- Sports equipment
- Child's watch
- Gift certificate to a favorite store

For the Mothers of the Bride and Groom

- A bracelet, earrings, or brooch
- Monogrammed compact
- Gift certificate for a spa treatment
- An evening bag
- Perfume
- Memory album including photos and other mementos

For the Fathers of the Bride and Groom

- Desk clock
- Tickets to theater or concert

- Golf accessories
- Restaurant gift certificate
- Beer- or Wine-of-the-Month Club subscription
- Flask
- Box of quality cigars

For the Bride

- Pearl necklace and/or bracelet
- Engraved locket
- Watch
- Hope chest
- Framed poem or love note

For the Groom

- Watch
- Cuff links
- Luggage
- Leather briefcase
- CDs or DVDs
- Scrapbook with photos and mementos from your life together

5

The Bridal Party

As we mentioned in the last chapter, you can think of your bridal party as the cast of a once-in-a-lifetime production: your wedding! The bridal party is there to help you and your fiancé—the glamorous leading lady and leading man—shine your brightest and enjoy every moment of your special day. If you've ever been in a wedding or have been married before, then you are probably familiar with the roles of some of the major players. If you're not sure exactly who does what, now is the perfect time to brush up on bridal party duties. After all, many people will look to you for guidance on their roles. Here's what you need to know to make sure everyone understands what is expected of them.

The Role of the Bride

Along with your groom, you, darling, are the star of the show! Your roles in this production are numerous: wedding coordinator, delighted guest, gracious hostess. While it's hard to sum up everything that you will do, your main responsibility is to work with your fiancé and whomever else you choose (often your parents and sometimes a wedding planner and other wedding professionals) to craft a nuptial ceremony and wedding reception that reflect you and your soon-to-be husband. Your exact to-do list will be dictated, in large part, by the type of wedding you have. A traditional church wedding, for instance, may involve focusing on tons of decisions, from music to flowers. A destination wedding, on the other hand, may mean you spend most of your time managing travel arrangements, but leave details like the cake and centerpieces to an on-site event coordinator.

Regardless of the style of wedding you've decided on, this is an exciting time, but also one that can be anxiety-provoking. After all, you'll be making lots of decisions (not the least of which is to spend the rest of your life with your fiancé!) and dealing with legions of people from parents to future in-laws to vendors. Keeping a cool head can be challenging at times, but it will help you avoid emotional blow-ups that you could regret long after your wedding day. Need a release? Turn to your bridal party—the women who know you best—for support. And don't underestimate the stress-busting potential of a night out with your girlfriends.

Here are some of the major responsibilities you have as the bride:

- Choosing a maid and/or matron of honor and bridesmaids (for advice on this, see chapter 1: "Getting Engaged").

- Selecting dresses for your attendants.

- Delegating wedding planning duties.

- Together with your groom, acting as a liaison between your families.

- Ensuring that your family creates a guest list and doesn't exceed their allowed number of guests.

- Planning a bridesmaids' luncheon, if you choose to host one (chapter 2: "Pre-Wedding Parties" gives you the lowdown on bridesmaids' luncheons).

- Selecting and purchasing gifts for your attendants (see chapter 4: "The Rehearsal Dinner" for gift ideas).

- Buying a wedding gift for your groom.

The Role of the Groom

It used to be that the bride and her mom were the main wedding planners and the groom pretty much just showed up at the church on the day of the wedding, but more and more grooms are putting their stamp on the day. If your fiancé is going to be intimately involved in wedding decisions, then he'll help research locations and wedding professionals, meet vendors, and finalize contracts. If he's less involved in the nitty-gritty, he can still help by facilitating communication between his family and you and your family. You and your groom should also try to present a united front and help each other through any difficulties that arise (think of it as good practice for when you are married).

Here are some other tasks that should be handled by the groom:

- Chooses the best man and the ushers (for more on selecting groomsmen, see chapter 1: "Getting Engaged").

- Assists with wedding planning tasks.

- Communicates wedding information to his family.

- Makes sure his family comes up with a guest list (and sticks to their allotted number of invites).

- Arranges and pays for the marriage license.

- Covers the cost of the officiant's fee.

- Reserves hotel rooms for wedding guests traveling in from out of town.

- Selects and pays for gifts for the groom's attendants. (Need some present ideas? Check out the suggestions in chapter 4: "The Rehearsal Dinner.")

- Chooses a gift for the bride.

- Makes honeymoon reservations. (Traditionally, the groom arranged and paid for the honeymoon himself, but these days many couples share the planning and the bill.)

Mother of the Bride

Traditionally, the mother of the bride took on the part of chief wedding planner. But these days, with many couples footing the bill for the wedding themselves or splitting the costs with their parents, Mom's role in the planning process has changed. While many mothers are still very involved, the extent to which they have decision-making power depends on the bride's relationship with her mom and how much she wants to include her.

Among the duties that mothers of the bride often fulfill:

Before the Wedding

- Hosts the first engagement party.

- Attends all showers planned in the bride's honor. (The mother of the bride can contribute to, but shouldn't host a bridal shower.)

- Assists the bride with wedding planning details.

- Selects her attire for the wedding and informs the groom's mother of her choice. (The bride's and groom's mothers will want their outfits to be similar in formality and complement each other well.)

- Shares a special item with the bride such as a piece of family jewelry she wore on her own wedding day, or provides her with all or some of the customary items for "something old, something new, something borrowed, something blue."

During the Ceremony

- Walks the bride down the aisle in some circumstances. It is customary at a Jewish wedding for both the mother and father of the bride to accompany her down the aisle, and some brides of other faiths are adopting this tradition. Also, if the father of the bride is deceased or not involved in the bride's life, the mother of the bride may escort her down the aisle in his place.

- Is the last person seated before the procession begins. She should be seated in the front row on the bride's side.

- May light a candle from which the bride will later light a unity candle with her groom.

During the Reception

- Stands in the receiving line with the bride and groom. The receiving line can take place immediately following the ceremony or as guests are arriving at the reception.

- May be announced at the reception just ahead of the groom's parents and the bridal party.

- Acts as the official hostess of the party by mingling and greeting guests.

Father of the Bride

Does the phrase "father of the bride" immediately bring to mind the Steve Martin character in the movie of the same name? If so, then you're thinking of the classic dad role. Traditionally, the father of the bride was the host of the wedding and, because he likely wrote the checks for the majority of the wedding expenses, he may have had a large say in wedding planning decisions. These days, the father of the bride's role has changed a bit because he may not be the sole financial contributor, but many of his duties—such as walking his daughter down the aisle—have remained.

Here's a look at what Dad can expect to do:

Before the Wedding

- May participate in wedding planning and decision making.

- May host the first engagement party—with Mom.

- May help out-of-town guests with their travel arrangements and accommodations.

- Gets fitted for formalwear to match or coordinate with the groom, groomsmen, and father of the groom.

- May attend the bachelor party.

- Escorts the bride to the ceremony.

During the Ceremony

- Walks the bride down the aisle. When the bride and her father reach the groom, the father often shakes hands with the groom and/or places the bride's hand in the groom's, lifts the bride's veil, and kisses her.

- Sits in the first pew with the mother of the bride. If they are divorced and not on great terms, the parent the bride is closest to sits in the first pew and the other parent sits in the third or fourth row with his or her new spouse, if he or she has remarried. (The rows between the parents are usually filled by siblings and grandparents.)

During the Reception

- May stand in the receiving line. If not, he can mingle with the guests instead.

- May be announced at the reception just ahead of the groom's parents and the bridal party.

- Shares a special father-daughter dance with the bride.

- May offer a toast to the newlyweds after the best man does.

- Works with the wedding venue staff to solve any problems that arise during the reception.

- Stays until the very end of the reception to say good night to the last guests and settle any outstanding bills with the wedding vendors.

Mother of the Groom

The mother of the groom, though she may not have as many duties as the bride's mother, is still an important part of the wedding. Depending on her relationship with her future daughter-in-law, she may be asked to participate in the wedding planning to some degree. At the least, she should be kept updated about the style of the wedding so she knows what to expect and how to dress.

Other mother of the groom duties include:

Before the Wedding

- Contacts the bride's family to arrange a get-together after the engagement is announced.

- Can help the bride and her parents put the engagement and wedding announcements in the groom's family's local newspaper.
- Attends bridal showers held in the bride's honor.
- Consults with bride's mother about wedding attire.
- Hosts the rehearsal dinner. If she and the groom's father are divorced, one or both of them can plan and pay for the rehearsal dinner.

During the Ceremony

- Along with the groom's father, she may walk the groom down the aisle as is customary in Jewish ceremonies.
- May light the candle from which the groom will later light the unity candle.

During the Reception

- Stands in the receiving line with the bride and groom and others.
- May be announced at the reception after the bride's parents but ahead of the bridal party
- Dances with her son to a special song.
- Mingles with guests.

Father of the Groom

Although the father of the groom may not be as visible as the father of the bride, he is still an honored guest at the wedding. He should receive a preferred seat at both the ceremony and reception, and he should take the opportunity to dance with the bride sometime during the night.

Before the Wedding

- Hosts the rehearsal dinner.
- Gets fitted for formal wear to match or coordinate with the groom, groomsmen, and father of the bride.
- May contribute to wedding costs.
- May attend the bachelor party.

During the Ceremony

- Sits in the front row on the groom's side.

During the Reception

- May stand in the receiving line. If not, he can mingle with the guests.
- May be announced into the reception after the bride's parents but ahead of the bridal party
- If paying for the wedding, he may act as host.
- Dances with the bride at some point during the reception.

Stepparents

Depending on their relationship to the bride or groom, stepparents may fulfill some or all of the duties traditionally expected of the parents. How do you assign tasks? Do whatever feels right for your particular situation. For example, if you are close with both your father and stepfather, both can walk you down the aisle, or each man can walk you part of the way. Divorced parents typically sit in separate rows during the ceremony and don't stand next to each other in the receiving line. Overall, consideration and communication can help everyone find a role they will feel comfortable with.

Ways to Remember a Loved One

You may wish to honor a deceased relative such as a parent, sibling, or grandparent. While you don't want to overshadow the happiness of the occasion, there are many nice ways to acknowledge a loved one.

- Mention the person in the wedding program. What to say is up to you, but a common sentiment is: "On this special day, we remember those who are with us in our hearts, including Mary Michaels, mother of the groom."

- Wear or carry something with sentimental meaning. A pocket watch, piece of jewelry, or handkerchief can be a tangible remembrance.

- Play a special song. You can include a song the person loved in the ceremony (you may want to note its significance in the program) or ask the band or DJ to play a particular song during the reception.

- Display photos. If one of your parents is deceased, it can be a sweet gesture to display a photo of your parents (perhaps on their wedding day) on a small table near the place card table at the reception.

- Make a donation in lieu of favors. Instead of giving guests a take-home item, consider making a donation to a charity or organization that was meaningful to your deceased relative.

The Role of the Maid or Matron of Honor

The maid or matron of honor (a "maid" of honor is a woman who is unmarried; a "matron" is a married woman), also known as an honor attendant, is the most important of the bridesmaids (think of her as the chief bridesmaid!). Usually the bride's sister or closest friend, she'll be your right-hand woman when it comes to all wedding-related matters. If you decide to have two maids or matrons of honor (or one of each) they can split the duties, although the maid of honor's role should take precedence during the ceremony—she would be the one to arrange your veil and train and hold your bouquet.

Before the Wedding

- Attends all prewedding events such as engagement party, showers, and bachelorette party.
- May plan the bridal shower and bachelorette party (the maid or matron of honor is not required to plan these events, but most do).
- Offers the bride emotional support as needed.
- Keeps a record of gifts given to the bride at the shower.
- Keeps bridesmaids updated on dress fittings and other bridal party details.
- Helps the bride with addressing invitation envelopes or any other tasks for which the bride needs assistance.

Bright Idea

A wedding newsletter—either on paper, via e-mail, or posted on a personal wedding website—is a terrific way to keep your wedding party updated on wedding-related happenings. You can include information such as pictures of the attire you've chosen for your bridesmaids and groomsmen, dress/tuxedo fitting schedules, and other important dates and details.

- Arrives at the bride's house (or other chosen location) for photos before the ceremony.

- Helps the bride dress for the ceremony.

During the Ceremony

- Arranges the bride's veil and train for the processional and recessional.

- Holds the bride's bouquet.

- Holds the groom's wedding band until the officiant asks for it.

- Signs the marriage license as a witness.

During the Reception

- Stands in the receiving line with the bride, groom, and their parents.

- May be announced by the emcee or bandleader as she enters the reception.

- May choose to give a toast to the newlyweds.

- Dances with the best man for the first dance.

- Is available for photos throughout the day.

Pays For

- Typically splits the bill for the bridal shower with the bridesmaids.

- Usually chips in with other bachelorette party guests to pay for the bride's night out.

- Her own dress, shoes, and accessories.

- Her travel and lodging (unless bride offers to pay).

The Role of the Bridesmaids

After the maid or matron of honor, the bridesmaids are usually the most important gals in your life and in your wedding. Besides showing up on your wedding day looking pretty, they may be called on during the wedding planning process to help out with a bridal shower, attend the bachelorette night, and pitch in on tasks from stuffing invitation envelopes to putting together party favors. These are your go-to girls!

Before the Wedding

- Helps the maid or matron of honor plan the shower and bachelorette party.
- Assists the bride with addressing invitations, assembling favors, and any other tasks.
- Offers the bride emotional support when needed.
- May have her hair and makeup done with the bride, although isn't necessarily required to.
- Arrives at the bride's house (or other chosen location) for photos before the ceremony.

During the Ceremony

- Walks in the processional and recessional.

During the Reception

- May be announced by the emcee or bandleader as she enters the reception.
- Dances with groomsman during the first dance.
- Mingles with guests.
- Is available for photos throughout the day.

Pays For

- Her own dress, shoes, and accessories.

- Often contributes to cost of bridal shower and bachelorette party.

- Her travel and lodging (unless bride offers to pay).

The Role of Junior Bridesmaids

Girls between the ages of nine and fourteen who are too young to be bridesmaids can be appointed junior bridesmaids. They often wear a dress that coordinates with, but is slightly different than, the dress the bridesmaids wear. Junior bridesmaids have many of the same duties as the bridesmaids but they don't

Can We Talk?

Q: I just found out that one of my bridesmaids will be six months pregnant when I get married. Can she still be in my wedding?

Dawn, 28, New Jersey

A: Sure! As long as you and your friend are comfortable with the idea, there's no reason for her to step down. If your pal lives far from your wedding location, however, it would be wise for her to check with her M.D. to make sure it's okay for her to travel. Ordering her dress may be a little trickier than usual, but an experienced dress shop pro should be able to guide her. Since it will be hard to know how much weight she will have gained by your wedding, she'll need to order her dress on the larger side and enlist a talented seamstress to tailor it closer to the wedding date. Also, look for styles specifically designed for pregnant attendants. Other than that, all she needs is a comfortable pair of shoes.

attend the bachelorette party or help pay for that party or the shower.

Before the Wedding

- Is available for dress fittings.
- Attends the bridal shower.

During the Ceremony

- Walks in the processional and recessional. The junior bridesmaid usually walks just ahead of the maid or matron of honor.

During the Reception

- May be announced by the emcee or bandleader as she enters the reception.

Pays For

- Traditionally, the junior bridesmaid's parents pay for her dress, shoes, and accessories.
- Parents usually pay for her travel and lodging (unless bride offers to pay).

Flower Girl

Young girls between the ages of four and eight years can make adorable flower girls. If you decide to ask a young relative or friend to be your flower girl, keep in mind that children are unpredictable. If you imagine your wedding as a perfectly orchestrated production, you may want to think twice about adding a child to the mix. The older the child is, the more likely she'll be able to carry off her duties.

Before the Wedding

• Gets fitted for a dress, accessories, and shoes.

During the Ceremony

• Walks down the aisle ahead of the bride during the processional. Some flower girls scatter flower petals in the bride's path, while others simply carry a bouquet, a basket of flowers, or a pomander.

During the Reception

• If the flower girl's parents decide it's appropriate, she may attend all or part of the reception.

Pays For

• Traditionally, the flower girl's parents buy her dress, shoes, and accessories.

• Parents pay for travel and lodging (unless bride offers to pay).

Bright Idea

If you have a very young flower girl or ring bearer, ask the parents to practice with the child ahead of time. They can make it a game where the child receives praise for performing her role correctly. Imagine the pride the child will feel when performing perfectly on the big day!

The Role of the Best Man

The best man, traditionally the groom's brother or best friend, has the most important role on the groom's "side" of the bridal party. Today, some grooms choose their fathers, close female friends, or two brothers or friends to fulfill this honor.

Before the Wedding

- Helps coordinate the groomsmen's attire and schedule fittings and clothing pickup (he also often takes charge of returning the groom's attire to the formalwear shop after the wedding).
- Plans the bachelor party.
- Makes sure the groom gets to the ceremony on time.
- Confirms the honeymoon travel arrangements.

During the Ceremony

- Ensures that all ushers are properly dressed.
- Holds the bride's wedding ring until the officiant asks for it.
- Signs the marriage license as a witness.
- Passes the envelope with the officiant's fee to the officiant after the ceremony.

During the Reception

- May be announced by the emcee or bandleader as he enters the reception.
- Gives the first toast at the reception.
- Dances the first dance with the maid or matron of honor.

Bright Idea

Keeping the wedding rings safe until the officiant asks for them is an important job! The best man should keep both the bride's and groom's ring in his pocket (check it thoroughly for holes first) since it could get stuck if he puts it on one of his fingers. Having the maid of honor hold the groom's ring isn't usually a good idea. Most dresses don't have pockets, and the maid of honor will have her hands full carrying her bouquet, holding the bride's bouquet, and fussing with the bride's train.

- Is available for photos.
- Makes sure the bride and groom's "getaway" car is ready.

Pays For

- Contributes to cost of bachelor party.
- Cost of clothing rental or purchase.
- Transportation and lodging (unless paid for by the groom).

The Role of Ushers (a.k.a. Groomsmen)

After the best man or best men, the groom can choose other close friends or relatives (or brothers of the bride, if there are any) to serve as ushers. The groom selects any number of ushers that he feels comfortable with, but remember there should be at least one usher for every fifty guests.

Did You Know?

When a female guest arrives, an usher should offer her his right arm and escort her to her seat. Her spouse or date should follow behind. Single male guests can simply be led to their seats. Ushers can determine a guest's seating preference by asking if she would like to be seated on the bride's side (in Catholic ceremonies, that would be on the left as you're looking at the altar; and for Jewish ceremonies on the right side) or the groom's side. If either the bride or the groom has many more guests than the other, the ushers can seat people so that they are evenly distributed on both sides of the aisle. Finally, if you are using pew or "within the ribbon" cards to indicate which guests should be seated closest to the front, inform your ushers so they know what to do when presented with a card.

Before the Wedding

- Helps the best man plan the bachelor party.
- Attends scheduled fittings for wedding attire.
- Picks up attire if it is a rental.

During the Ceremony

- Arrives early.
- Seats guests as they arrive.

During the Reception

- May be announced by the emcee or bandleader as he enters the reception.
- Dances with bridesmaid during the first dance.

- Mingles with wedding guests.
- Is available for photos.

Pays For

- Contributes to cost of bachelor party.
- Cost of clothing rental or purchase.
- Transportation and lodging (unless paid for by the groom).

The Role of the Ring Bearer

A young boy between four and eight years old can take on the ceremonial role of ring bearer. His job: to walk down the aisle either alongside or just ahead of the flower girl, carrying a pillow with two wedding bands tied to it. For safekeeping, the best man usually holds the actual wedding rings while the ring bearer carries symbolic replicas on his pillow.

Before the Wedding

- Gets fitted for his wedding attire.

During the Ceremony

- Walks in the processional and recessional.

During the Reception

- If his parents decide it's appropriate, he may attend all or part of the reception.

Pays For

- Traditionally, the ring bearer's parents pay for his clothing.
- Parents pay for transportation and lodging (unless bride or groom offers to pay).

What to Wear

Your wedding will probably be one of the biggest—if not the biggest—fashion moments in your life, so you will no doubt spend plenty of time browsing through racks of dresses and deciding what look is right for you. When it comes to choosing clothing for yourself, your groom, and your bridal party, there is one guiding principle to keep in mind: Select attire that matches the formality and style of your wedding and is appropriate for the time of day you'll marry. Traditional church or synagogue weddings, for example, generally call for formal wear, while a laid-back outdoor ceremony usually warrants more casual garb. Check out the charts below to determine what's right for your wedding time and tone.

Daytime Wedding Wear

Outfit yourself, your groom, and the bridal party based on these selections if your wedding will be before 6 P.M.

ULTRA-FORMAL	
Bride	Floor-length gown, long train, gloves, and veil.
Bridesmaids	Floor-length or tea-length dresses (hemline hits the leg midcalf), gloves, matching shoes. May wear jeweled combs or other hair accessories.
Groom/Groomsmen	*Traditional*: A cutaway long coat with striped trousers, wing-collar shirt, ascot, and vest. *Contemporary*: Long or short contoured tuxedo with wing-collar shirt and black accessories.

FORMAL

Bride	Floor-length gown (hemline falls 1 to 1½ inches from the floor), long train, gloves, and veil.
Bridesmaids	Floor-length or tea-length dresses and shoes to match. May wear jeweled combs or other hair accessories and gloves.
Groom/Groomsmen	*Traditional*: Stroller, waistcoat, striped trousers, white shirt, and striped tie. *Contemporary*: Formal tuxedo with a dress shirt, bow or four-in-hand tie, vest, or cummerbund.

SEMI-FORMAL

Bride	Floor-length or shorter gown and short veil.
Bridesmaids	Tea-length or shorter dresses with shoes and accessories to match.
Groom/Groomsmen	*Traditional*: Formal suit with a white, colored, or striped shirt and a four-in-hand tie. *Contemporary*: Dinner jacket or formal suit with dress shirt, bow or four-in-hand tie, vest, or cummerbund.

INFORMAL

Bride	Sundress, suit, cocktail dress, or pantsuit. A veil or hat is optional.
Bridesmaids	Short dress or suit, similar in style to the bride's.
Groom/Groomsmen	*Traditional*: Suit with a white, colored, or striped shirt and a four-in-hand tie. *Contemporary*: Dinner jacket or formal suit, dress shirt, bow or four-in-hand tie, vest.

Evening Wedding Wear

Planning an after-six affair? Here's the lowdown on the right looks for the wedding party.

ULTRA-FORMAL	
Bride	Floor-length gown, long train, gloves, and veil.
Bridesmaids	Floor-length or tea-length dresses, gloves, matching shoes. May wear jeweled combs or other hair accessories.
Groom/Groomsmen	*Traditional*: Full-dress tailcoat, matching trousers, white waistcoat, white bow tie, wing-collar shirt. *Contemporary*: Long or short contoured tuxedo with formal trousers, wing-collar shirt.

FORMAL	
Bride	Floor-length gown, long train, veil, and gloves.
Bridesmaids	Floor-length or tea-length dresses, gloves, matching shoes and accessories.
Groom/Groomsmen	*Traditional*: Stroller, waistcoat, striped trousers, white shirt, and striped tie. *Contemporary*: Tuxedo, dress shirt, bow or four-in-hand tie, vest, or cummerbund.

SEMI-FORMAL	
Bride	Floor-length or shorter gown and short veil.
Bridesmaids	Floor-length, tea-length, or shorter dresses, matching shoes and accessories.
Groom/Groomsmen	*Traditional*: Tuxedo or dinner jacket, dress shirt, bow tie, vest, or cummerbund. *Contemporary*: Dinner jacket or formal suit, dress shirt, bow or four-in-hand tie, vest.

INFORMAL	
Bride	Short dress or suit, veil or hat optional.
Bridesmaids	Short dresses or suits, similar in style to the bride's.
Groom/Groomsmen	*Traditional*: Suit with white, colored, or striped shirt and four-in-hand tie. *Contemporary*: Dinner jacket or formal suit, dress shirt, bow or four-in-hand tie, vest, or cummerbund.

Men's Wear Variations

Don't know a stroller from a waistcoat? Relax—most people don't! Check out the definitions below to demystify common formalwear lingo.

Cutaway coat: Also known as a morning coat, the cutaway tapers from the front waist button to a long, wide back tail. This jacket style, which is longer in the back than it is in the front, is worn for a traditional, ultra-formal daytime wedding.

Stroller: Also called a walking coat, this style is cut slightly longer than a regular suit jacket. It is the traditional attire choice for a formal daytime wedding

Tuxedo: A single- or double-breasted jacket with matching trousers that is worn for formal or semiformal evening weddings.

Dinner suit: A white or ivory jacket with black formal trouser. It is worn for formal and semiformal evening weddings in warm weather.

Tailcoat jacket: This style comes in black and white and is short in the front with two long back tails.

Bow tie: A tie in the shape of a bow that is available in a variety of widths, colors, and patterns to match the vest or cummerbund.

Wing-collar shirt: This style shirt features a stiff band that encircles the neck with turned-down points (the "wings") in front.

Ascot: A wide necktie that is looped over and held in place under the chin with a tie tack or a stickpin. Also known as a cravat, an ascot is worn with a wing-collar shirt, a daytime cutaway jacket, or a traditional tuxedo.

Four-in-hand: A standard long, knotted necktie. A four-in-hand is the official name for the type of tie most people consider a "regular" tie.

Cummerbund: A pleated sash made of silk or satin that is worn at the waist to cover the trousers' waistband. It is only worn with a bow tie, never with a four-in-hand tie.

Vest/Waistcoat: Can be worn in place of a cummerbund to hide the trousers' waistband. It is often worn with a coordinating four-in-hand tie or bow tie.

What Not to Wear

Tying the knot for the second or more time? It's a good idea to skip the blusher veil—the piece that covers the bride's face as she walks down the aisle. Though the "rules" about what a pre-viously married bride should wear have relaxed dramatically, blushers are still considered to be best only for first-time or very young brides. You can wear a veil sans the blusher, or go for a tiara, hat, or a few fresh flowers pinned in your hair. All are beautiful choices.

Attire Options for Parents

Are Mom and Dad unsure about just how dressed up they should be? The answer is simple: They should match the level or for-mality of the rest of the wedding party. If the bride and bridesmaid are going ultra-formal, then so should the mothers of the bride and the groom. If everyone is opting for a more casual look with, say, skirt suits or sundresses, then the moms should follow that trend. That said, parents should wear some-thing they will feel at ease in. A mother who hates to wear dresses may consider donning a formal pantsuit instead, if she would be more comfortable. And these days, pretty much any color goes, even black and white. One exception: White dresses that are too bride-like are a no-no. If a dress could possibly be mistaken for a wedding gown, Mom should keep shopping.

Traditionally, the mother of the bride picks her dress first and then calls the mother of the groom to let her know what she's chosen—that way, their looks can be complemen-tary without being too similar. Most moms today don't follow this tradition too strictly, though. Still, if your mom wants to touch base with your fiancé's mom, she's welcome to do that. In fact, it's good insurance against the two of them unknow-ingly arriving in the same outfit and looking like their own mini-bridal party! As for the dads, dressing is pretty easy: They can wear attire that is the same as or similar to what the groomsmen are wearing.

Dressing Young Attendants

The younger members of your bridal party—the junior bridesmaid, junior groomsmen, flower girl, and ring bearer—should be dressed to complement the rest of the group. It's best not to dress young girls in the same dress as the bridesmaids, however, since that will often be a look that is too sophisticated for a youngster. For junior bridesmaids, select a dress in the same color and fabric as the bridesmaids' dresses, in a silhouette that is flattering on a young girl. Flower girls traditionally wear a dress with a full skirt and pouf sleeves in white, ivory, or a pastel or other color that complements the bridal party. For instance, if the bridesmaids are wearing lavender dresses, the flower girl can also wear lavender or she can wear a white dress with a lavender sash.

Can We Talk?

Q: My fiancé wants to ask his best friend, who lives in another state, to be his best man. Are we expected to pay for his flight and hotel stay?

Robin, 32, Nevada

A: Figuring out who pays for what can certainly be confusing. Traditionally, the groom and his family picked up the tab for the groom's attendants' hotel accommodations, but not the cost of travel—that was up to each groomsman. More common today is that each member of the bridal party funds his or her own lodging and travel costs. That said, if you and your fiancé are concerned about the strain on his friend's budget, your fiancé can offer to pay for the hotel room or for another wedding-related expense such as the formalwear rental. No doubt his friend will appreciate your generous gesture.

A junior groomsman can wear a tuxedo to match the rest of the groom's attendants. The traditional attire for a ring bearer is short pants and a jacket, but he could also wear a blazer, suit, or a child-sized tuxedo to match the groomsmen.

Treat Your Bridal Party Well

It's easy to get caught up in the excitement of your wedding and start issuing orders and making diva-like demands—after all, there is so much that needs to be done. The problem: Though your friends will probably be willing to overlook your, umm, enthusiasm to a certain extent, too high expectations can make even the most patient pals bristle. Treat your attendants right, and you'll end up with a beautiful wedding—and all of your friendships intact.

- **Be flexible.** True, it's your wedding and you should do things the way you and your fiancé prefer, but sometimes it pays to be flexible. Does a bridesmaid want to get her hair done by her own stylist instead of the one you selected? It may not hurt to let her do her own thing.

- **Don't be too demanding.** It's one thing to expect your bridesmaids to wear the dress you select for them, it's entirely different (and, let's be honest, over the top) to expect them to wear the exact shade of nail polish and lipstick you decree. Being overly demanding can turn your pals off just when you need to depend on them the most.

- **Be reasonable about time commitments.** Your wedding is of course important to your bridesmaids and ushers, but they still have their own work and family obligations. So while it's fine to ask the girls to help you assemble wedding favors one afternoon, it's insensitive to expect them to spend every Saturday for two months on wedding preparation.

- **Be budget-conscious.** Being in a wedding can get expensive, between the dress, the shoes, chipping in for the shower, and so on. When possible, try to be sensitive to price and choose an option that won't put unnecessary stress on your bridal party's wallets.

- **Be appreciative.** A sincere in-person "thanks" or a brief mailed or e-mailed note of gratitude after your pal has gone out of her way to help—say, by spending an afternoon helping you make ceremony programs—can make your party members feel appreciated.

Dealing with Difficult Attendants

Yes, you chose them because they're your favorite people on earth, but from time to time even those dearest to us can drive us nuts. If you find that one of your attendants is being less than enthusiastic—or even downright uncooperative—you must address the matter as soon as possible, or risk a blow-up. Understand that your friend might regret accepting your invitation to be in the wedding party because it requires more time and money than she'd realized, or maybe she's jealous of all the attention you're getting. Whatever the reason, invite her out for coffee and a talk. Say something like, "I've noticed you don't seem happy about the dress I've chosen [or whatever describes your situation]. Is there something I can do to change that?" Hopefully, she'll open up and the matter will be resolved. But if things heat up, it may be time to give her an "out." Say, "Would you like to step down as bridesmaid? If so, I understand. Is that what you want to do?" If she is really unhappy enough to back out, you've politely given her a way to do it—and your friendship will be saved.

6

The Marriage Ceremony

The Marriage Ceremony

The ceremony is arguably the most important part of your wedding day—it's the time where you are transformed from an engaged couple to husband and wife. Since you'll remember saying your "I do's" for the rest of your life, it's important to carefully plan a ceremony that will be meaningful for both of you. With so many other details to tend to—the reception, the dresses, the flowers—it can be tempting to assume the ceremony will take care of itself, but make time to carefully select your music, readings, and participants and you'll be glad you did.

Your Ceremony Style

The first decision you need to make is what style ceremony you prefer. Maybe it's a no-brainer, and you've always known that you would wed in the hometown church your family has attended for years. Or perhaps there's no doubt in your mind that you want to exchange vows barefoot on the beach in Maui. If you know exactly what you're after, great, you can start planning your dream ceremony. But if you're unsure whether to go the religious or secular route, or you don't have a particular ceremony location in mind, read on for help in finding the right place for you. Remember: Your choice of ceremony locations is virtually limitless. You can tie the knot in a forest, a park, a planetarium, a museum, or a private home. Some folks have even done it underwater or in space!

Following are some of the most common ceremony options, and the pluses and minuses of each.

Religious Ceremony in a House of Worship

This is a traditional wedding ceremony performed by a priest, rabbi, or minister taking place in a church, temple, or other house of worship.

Benefits

- The officiant is likely experienced with weddings and can guide you through the process.

- Your ceremony will include many familiar traditions.

- You may use established vows, rather than having to write your own.

- Your officiant can provide a selection of songs and readings from which to choose.

- Musical accompaniment for your ceremony is often easily arranged through your officiant or house of worship.

Potential Drawbacks

- Less flexibility in scheduling your ceremony because most houses of worship will only have weddings on certain days and at certain times.

- Fewer opportunities to personalize your ceremony because there are usually approved readings and music from which you must choose.

- You may have to meet specific requirements such as completing premarital counseling (for example, the Catholic Church requires this).

- There may be rules regarding music, photography, décor, or even the style of gown you wear.

Religious Ceremony in Another Venue

This type of ceremony consists of a religious service performed by a clergy member at a location of your choosing. For example, a rabbi might perform your ceremony in a room at your reception hall.

Benefits

- You still retain the religious aspects of the ceremony that are important to you and/or your family.

- The officiant is likely experienced with weddings and can help you plan your ceremony.

- You can usually decorate the room however you like.

- Your ceremony and reception can be conveniently in one place.

Potential Drawbacks

- Many priests won't perform a wedding ceremony outside of the walls of a church, so if having a priest officiate is important to you, you may not have the option of where to hold your ceremony.

- You will probably have to have your song and reading selections approved by your officiant.

Ecumenical Ceremony

A good option for interfaith couples, an ecumenical ceremony often includes a clergy member from each of the participating faiths—say, a rabbi and a minister when a Jewish woman marries a Protestant man—and blends the traditions of both religions.

Benefits

- Allows both partners' faiths to be represented.
- Provides the opportunity for more customatization than a traditional one-religion ceremony.
- Includes readings and symbols that may be important to each family, like the breaking of the glass in a Jewish wedding or the lighting of a unity candle in a Christian ceremony.

Potential Drawbacks

- You may have some difficulty finding clergy members willing to participate if they feel strongly about only performing single-faith ceremonies.
- Extra research and planning are necessary since the ceremony won't follow a strict religious format.

Civil Ceremony

Usually performed by a judge, justice of the peace, mayor, county clerk, or other official, a civil ceremony doesn't involve a member of the clergy or take place in a house of worship. Since you essentially create the ceremony to your own specifications, it can be as long or as short as you choose.

Benefits

- Good choice for couples of different religions or those who don't want a traditional religious ceremony.

- You can design the ceremony to reflect your own preferences.

- You can choose a nontraditional location such as a beach or mountaintop.

- No limits on the readings (poems, etc.) or music (jazz, top 40, country) used in your ceremony.

- Can include a spiritual, but nonreligious, component.

- You can usually decorate the room however you like.

Potential Drawbacks

- You need to find both a location and an officiant.

- Instead of following a set format, you'll need to design your entire ceremony.

- Some family members may balk at a secular ceremony.

Ceremony Site Checklist

Whatever style ceremony you decide on, you will need to select and book a wedding site. If you choose to get married in your own church or temple, then you won't be visiting and evaluating a number of sites. Still, you'll want to get some basic information to make sure that your ceremony site will mesh with the plans you have. Consider these issues when visiting ceremony locations:

___ *Large enough to hold the number of guests we expect*

___ *Available for the date and time we want*

___ *Parking adequate for our guests*

___ *We meet the officiant's requirements*

___ *The fee is within our budget*

___ *We feel comfortable with the officiant, or we're able to bring in an officiant of our choice*

___ *We are comfortable with any music, photography, décor, or attire restrictions*

___ *Site is accessible for all guests*

___ *Available for rehearsal in advance of our wedding*

The following issues may not be deal breakers, but are things that are good to know up front. Be sure to ask these questions:

___ *Are any other weddings or events scheduled for our date? (Some places book weddings for different times on the same day, and you don't want to feel rushed.)*

___ *Does the location provide services like set up, clean up, and parking?*

___ *What are the fees for any musicians who are affiliated with the site?*

___ *Can we or our florist get in to decorate before the ceremony?*

Can We Talk?

Q: There is a picture-perfect church a few towns away from where I live that would be a beautiful place to have my wedding ceremony. However, I'm not a member of this church. Can I still wed there?

Katherine, 26, Maryland

A: Every church has its own rules and requirements for weddings, so you'll need to contact a clergy member at the church you're interested in. But first you'll want to clarify the church's affiliation with your religion. For example, if you're Catholic and you're interested in a Presbyterian church, it will be a no-go. Also, know that some clergy members resent "church shopping" and will only perform weddings for couples who are already (or at least one person is already) members of the congregation. The exception: Many college chapels will marry alumni even if they aren't currently members of that congregation. Still, if the church you love is one you're thinking of joining as a parishioner, ask the priest about requirements.

Consider Your Guests When Choosing a Location

As a gracious host, you'll want to do everything you can to make the day comfortable and enjoyable for all of your guests. If you expect a number of elderly people or people who have difficulty getting around, keep them in mind when choosing your ceremony location. Often, you can arrange to have them dropped off near the entrance to the ceremony if the parking is far away. Alternatively, some locations such as country clubs and resorts may have golf carts available to ferry guests who are unable to walk long distances. Similarly, if a friend or family member uses a wheelchair, be sure that your ceremony location is accessible—and that you tell the guest where he or she may enter. Also, alert an usher to the location of a special entrance (if it's not obvious) so he is prepared to assist your guests as needed.

Planning an Interfaith Ceremony

Planning your ceremony when you and your fiancé are of different faiths can be challenging, but it's certainly doable. The most important thing: Stay flexible and keep the lines of communication open. Start by visiting each other's churches or temples and familiarizing yourself with the rituals of each religion. One of the benefits of an interfaith, or ecumenical, service is that you can divide the ceremony equally between the elements of each religion. You can also pick a "neutral" ceremony location—a ballroom, garden, or restaurant, for example—so that neither family feels it's on the other's turf. Alternatively, one of your officiants may be willing to host at his or her location and invite the other clergy member to participate in the ceremony. For instance, a Protestant minister may be willing to officiate your wedding in his church, assisted by a Catholic priest. Talk to your clergy members about your situation, or look for an ecumenical clergy member (check magazine or newspaper advertisements or inquire at a theological seminary). Also, *Joining Hands and Hearts: Interfaith, Intercultural Wedding Celebrations, A Practical Guide for Couples* by Rev. Susanna Stefanachi Macomb is a great resource for ceremony planning ideas as well as information on various religious traditions.

Working with Your Officiant

Once your ceremony location is secured, it's time to start working with your officiant to design your wedding ceremony. The style of wedding you are planning may determine how much interaction you have with your officiant. A Catholic church wedding will usually entail several meetings, but you'll spend much less time with your officiant if you're planning a civil wedding. A few rules of etiquette can help you maintain a good relationship with your officiant:

- First and foremost, be respectful to your officiant and the rules of the house of worship. It can be frustrating to find out that you can't do everything your own way (especially if you've gotten used to calling the shots for reception details).

- Be sensitive to matters of time. It's reasonable to check in with your officiant periodically with questions or concerns about the ceremony; it's not reasonable to expect your officiant to function like a wedding planner who is paid to carry out your wishes. Also, be punctual on the day of your wedding so that your officiant and guests aren't waiting around, and so you don't interfere with any other events scheduled at your location.

- ¥ Give an appropriate amount for the officiant's fee. The fee is usually at your discretion, and most people determine the amount based on how well they know the officiant and how involved he has been in the marriage preparation and wedding planning. Typically, an amount of $50 and up is acceptable.

- ¥ Arrange for your groom or best man to give the officiant his fee after the wedding ceremony. The proper way to do it: Place the payment and a note of thanks in a sealed envelope addressed to the officiant.

- Invite your officiant (and his or her spouse, if applicable) to attend your reception.

Ceremony Basics

Regardless of your religion or the type of ceremony you choose, there are certain elements—music, readings, and vows—that are fairly universal. Find out more about each of these important components below.

Musical Notes

The music you select contributes greatly to the tone of your ceremony and literally provides a soundtrack for your wedding. Ceremony music is divided into three parts:

The prelude: Soft background music that begins thirty to forty-five minutes before the start of the ceremony and continues as guests arrive and are seated. Classical selections are often chosen.

> ***Popular selections:*** Stookey's *The Wedding Song*, Bach's *Jesu, Joy of Man's Desiring*, Handel's *Pastoral Symphony*, Mendelssohn's *Adagio*.

The processional: This is the music that accompanies the bridal party as they proceed into the ceremony. Selections are usually upbeat and reminiscent of a majestic march. Many couples choose two songs for the processional: the first for the bridal party and the second for the bride and her escort.

> ***Popular selections:*** Pachelbel's *Canon in D*, Schubert's *Ave Maria*, Clarke's *Trumpet Voluntary* and *The Prince of Denmark's March*, Wagner's *Bridal Chorus* (the tune we know as "Here Comes the Bride"), Mendelssohn's *Wedding March*.

The recessional: Often a festive march, these tunes mark the joyous conclusion of the ceremony and accompany you on your first walk as husband and wife.

> ***Popular selections:*** Beethoven's *Ode to Joy*, Vivaldi's *Four Seasons*, Edward Elgar's *Pomp and Circumstance no. 4*, Handel's *Water Music Suite*, Willan's *Finale Jubilante*.

Hiring Musicians

Different ceremony locations handle the selection of music and commissioning of musicians in different ways. Some houses of worship have musicians and singers on staff. At others, you will need to hire independent professionals. Your officiant or location manager can guide you.

First, you'll want to find out if your church or temple has musicians with whom you are required to work. Many churches, for example, require you to use their organist. If you would like other instrumentalists, for example, a trumpeter or violinist to accompany the church's organist, talk to your officiant or the director of music to make arrangements. He or she may be able to recommend people with whom they've worked before. Fees vary, so find out that information up front.

If you have a friend or family member with a beautiful voice, asking her to sing at your wedding can be a nice way to personalize your ceremony. Unlike professional musicians you hire, it's not appropriate to pay a friend or relative for singing. Instead, a nice gift would be a better way to express your gratitude.

Using Prerecorded Music

Some couples opt to forgo live music in favor of prerecorded songs. This option is much less costly and lets you choose from a huge selection of songs and arrangements. If you choose to use CDs in place of live music, talk to your officiant or location manager about the logistics. Who will be responsible for setup? Who will man the CD player, stopping and starting it at appropriate times? Also, be sure to do at least one run-through with the music. Unlike live musicians who can start and stop seamlessly on cue, a recorded song's length isn't flexible. Be sure the tune is long enough to get you down the aisle, but not so long that it continues on awkwardly or has to be stopped abruptly.

Did You Know?

Many churches don't allow the inclusion of Wagner's *Bridal Chorus*—the tune most of us recognize as "Here comes the bride..."—in the wedding ceremony. Their reason: The piece is not religious music; it is from the opera *Lohengrin.*

Readings

The readings you choose are an important part of your service, and the amount of leeway you have in selecting them will depend upon your officiant's rules. Some religions allow more flexibility than others. In some cases, your officiant might provide you with a list of approved readings from which you select those that most appeal to you. Often, if you have another reading in mind, you can seek your officiant's approval for that reading. In most religious ceremonies, the readings will come from scripture. In secular or ecumenical ceremonies, you can often include a favorite poem or song lyric about love or marriage. For ideas, check out the book *The 100 Best Love Poems Of All Time* or **www.poetry.com**, where you'll find classics by poets such as Elizabeth Barrett Browning ("How do I love thee? Let me count the ways"), William Shakespeare ("Shall I compare thee to a summer's day? Thou art more lovely and more temperate"), and Anne Bradstreet ("If ever two were one then surely we. If ever man were lov'd by wife, then thee") as well as works by Robert Browning, Emily Dickinson, and Alfred, Lord Tennyson.

A nice way to honor loved ones who aren't in your bridal party is to ask them to do a reading. They don't have to participate in your wedding rehearsal, but it's thoughtful to provide them with a copy of the reading in advance, when possible.

Vows and Exchange of Rings

In many ways, your vows and ring exchange are the essence of the wedding ceremony. Depending on how strict your officiant is, you may be able to customize these parts of your service to make it a unique reflection of you and your fiancé. Many couples choose to recite the traditional vows that have been exchanged for hundreds of years (and which vary a bit by religion and house of worship). Others opt to write their own vows expressing their personal feelings and promises.

Did You Know?

Often, brides will wear their engagement ring on their right hand so the groom can easily slip on her wedding band. She can then switch her engagement ring back to her left hand once the wedding band is on.

How to Write Your Own Vows

Penning your own heartfelt vows is a great way to personalize your ceremony. You can say something serious, sentimental, lighthearted, or a combination of those—whatever best suits your and your fiancé's personalities. If the idea of writing your own vows appeals to you, but the thought of actually putting pen to paper is daunting, give yourself plenty of time (the night before your wedding isn't the time to sit down and start) and keep these pointers in mind.

- **Decide whether your vows will be "his" and "hers" or "ours."** You and your groom can each write your vows separately—you can share them in advance to make sure they match in style, tone, and length, or you can hear each other's words for the first time at your wedding—or you can work together to come up with one set of vows that you will both recite.

- **Cover the key components.** Your vows represent an agreement between you and your future husband. As such, they should include three important parts: a declaration of love ("Adam, my darling, my love for you is enormous and eternal"); promises for your marriage ("I promise to be your best friend and strongest supporter"); and personal touches ("Loving you has changed my life and made me look forward to our future").

- **Select a style.** Though you can each write from your own heart, the style of your vows (serious versus humorous and so on) should be similar.

- **Seek out inspiration.** Poetry or romantic prose can put you in the right mind-set and stimulate your creativity. Check out books such as *Weddings from the Heart* by Daphne Rose Kingma for ideas. You can also see sample vows at **www.celebrantusa.com**.

- **Keep them short and sweet.** Limit your vows to between one and three minutes each.

- **Avoid anything too risqué.** Keep in mind that your vows will be said publicly in front of your family and friends. Save intimate details for when you and your new hubby are alone.

- **Get comfortable with your words.** Practice your vows a few times before your wedding—but be careful not to sound so rehearsed that your words seem unnatural. If you need to have note cards at the ceremony that's fine. After all, it can be hard to keep your thoughts straight when you're so emotional!

The Order of the Day

Now that you're familiar with some of the major parts of a wedding ceremony, it's time to turn to the details. You may have attended dozens of weddings, but when it comes to remembering what happened in which order, the specifics may be kind of cloudy. No problem: The line-ups below show the traditional order of the main events leading up to the ceremony.

Christian Ceremony Order

1. *Ushers arrive one hour before the ceremony is scheduled to begin.*

2. *Guests arrive and are seated by the ushers.*

3. *Grandparents and other honored guests are seated.*

4. *The groom's parents are seated.*

5. *The bride's mother is seated (unless she is walking her daughter down the aisle).*

6. *The aisle runner is unrolled, if one is being used.*

7. *The priest takes his place at the altar.*

8. *The groom and best man enter from a side door or behind the altar and stand at the altar.*

9. *The bridal party procession begins.*

Jewish Ceremony Order

1. *Ushers arrive one hour before the ceremony is scheduled to begin.*

2. *Guests arrive and are seated by the ushers.*

3. *The procession begins, led by the cantor and rabbi.*

Here Comes the Bride

Once the music starts, it's time for your big entrance! For religious ceremonies, a traditional order of procession is almost always followed. There is no standard order of procession for a civil or ecumenical ceremony, but you can adopt these setups to fit your needs.

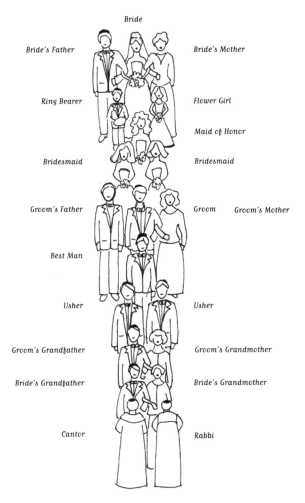

There may be more than one set of grandparents on each side, in which case one pair can follow the other. The bridesmaids may walk alone or in pairs.

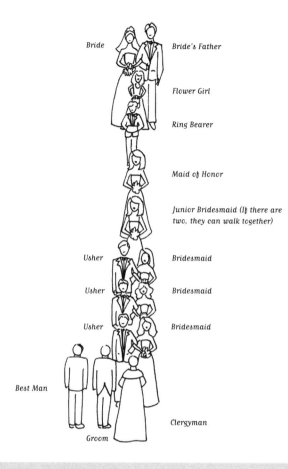

Bride

Bride's Father

Flower Girl

Ring Bearer

Maid of Honor

Junior Bridesmaid (If there are two, they can walk together)

Usher

Bridesmaid

Usher

Bridesmaid

Usher

Bridesmaid

Best Man

Clergyman

Groom

Did You Know?

Movie weddings often feature two ushers dramatically unrolling a white aisle runner before the bridesmaids and brides walk down the aisle. In reality, some houses of worship and other venues discourage (or even forbid) the use of the white carpet for fear of someone tripping on it. If your location allows an aisle runner, and you plan to use one (be sure to walk very carefully), run through the unrolling at your rehearsal so the designated ushers have the move down smoothly (just be sure no one walks on it so that it stays clean for the big day!).

Bridal Party Positions

Once the wedding party has entered the ceremony area, there's the issue of where to sit or stand. Etiquette dictates certain positions for each member of the bridal party, but these setups may vary depending on your individual circumstances. For example, sometimes the entire bridal party stands at the altar or under the huppah. Other times, only the honor attendants do, while the others sit or stand off to the side or in the first pew at a church. Here's a peek at the most common arrangements for Christian and Jewish weddings:

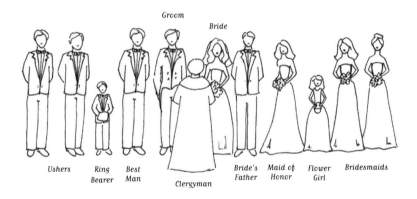

Ushers   Ring   Best   Bride's Maid of Flower Bridesmaids
         Bearer Man   Father   Honor   Girl
              Clergyman

Groom Bride

Bridesmaids   Ushers

Cantor   Rabbi

Bride's Father   Bride's Mother   Maid of Honor   Bride   Groom   Best Man   Groom's Mother   Groom's Father

Recessional

Once the ceremony has concluded and the recessional music has begun, it's time to move on. You should exit in the following order:

For a Christian Ceremony

1. *Bride and groom, with the bride holding the groom's right arm.*

2. *The flower girl and the ring bearer (the flower girl should be on the ring bearer's right).*

3. *The maid or matron of honor and the best man, with the woman holding the man's right arm. (If there are two maids or matrons of honor and one best man, each woman can hold an arm and they can walk as a trio.)*

4. *Bridesmaids and ushers (groomsmen) walk in pairs (determine in advance how they will pair up), with the bridesmaid holding the usher's right arm. If there is an odd number of ushers, one can walk alone. If there are two more ushers than bridesmaids, the ushers can walk side by side. If there are more bridesmaids than ushers, ushers can escort a bridesmaid on each arm.*

5. *Following traditional etiquette, ushers should walk to the front of the church to escort the mothers of the bride and groom and any other honored guests. However, these days parents and guests often file out behind the bridal party and are escorted by their spouses or companions.*

6. *Guests exit row by row starting with those closest to the altar.*

For a Jewish Ceremony

1. *Bride and groom, with the bride holding the groom's left arm.*

2. *The bride's parents, with the mother holding the father's left arm.*

3. *The groom's parents, with the mother holding the father's left arm.*

4. *The flower girl and the ring bearer (the flower girl should be on the ring bearer's left side).*

5. *The maid or matron of honor on the best man's left arm.*

6. *Bridesmaids holding ushers' left arms.*

7. *The rabbi and the cantor (the cantor should walk on the rabbi's left side).*

Did You Know?

If you wear gloves down the aisle, it is proper to remove them once you reach the altar or huppah and pass them, along with your bouquet, to your maid of honor. She will hold them throughout the ceremony. You can put your gloves back on after the recessional so that you can wear them into the reception. If your bridesmaids are wearing gloves, they can keep them on for the entire ceremony. Another option for the bride: Wear gloves that have a cutout on the ring finger to allow for you to put on your ring without removing your gloves.

Get with the Program

If you're still confused by the rules of what happens when during your ceremony, imagine how your guests will feel! To help them stay on track, consider distributing wedding programs. A wedding program is basically a guide to your wedding ceremony. It lets guests know who is involved and in what order things will happen. While not required, it is a nice way to make your guests feel included in your ceremony and a great opportunity to show off your creativity. If you are having an interfaith wedding, or expect many guests who may be unfamiliar with certain religious or ethnic rituals, the program is a good place to provide a brief explanation so guests can appreciate the meaning behind the symbols.

Your program can take any format you choose: a single page or card, a multi-page booklet, a scroll that guests unroll, and so on. It's best to keep your program similar in style to the rest of your wedding. It's also nice to coordinate the program with your invitations and other stationery. You can carry through your wedding colors in the program, if you like. Likewise, the contents of your program are up to you. Some of the things you'll want to consider including:

- Bride and groom's names

- Wedding date.

- Wedding location.

- The parts of the ceremony and the order in which they will occur.

- Words for prayers, if you wish your guests to recite them along with you.

- The names of those involved in the ceremony, including parents, the bridal party, readers, singers, and officiants.

- Reading selections and their origins.

- Names of the musical selections and their composers and/or performers.

- A quote, poem, or song lyric that is meaningful to you and your fiancé.

- A mention of deceased loved ones you wish to honor.

- A note of thanks to your parents and others who are special to you.

- Explanations of religious or ethnic rituals.

Programs can be distributed to guests as they arrive by a designated program attendant. This is a good job for a friend or relative whom you wish to include in a special way. It can even be done by a well-behaved school-age child or preteen. Another option: Place a program on each guest's seat (a friend or usher can do this) before the guests arrive.

Sample Wedding Program

There are many variations on the wedding program. Here is just one way you can do it, beginning with the cover:

The Marriage Ceremony

of

Amy Beth Jenkins

and

David Richard Hornsby

Saturday, the sixteenth of April
Two thousand and five

St. Helen's Church
New York City

Inside Pages

The Wedding Party

Officiant	*Father William O'Donnell*
Parents of the Bride	*Mr. and Mrs. Adam Jenkins*
Parents of the Groom	*Mr. and Mrs. Richard Hornsby*
Maid of Honor	*Annabelle Jenkins, Sister of the Bride*
Best Man	*Steven Hornsby, Brother of the Groom*
Bridesmaids	*Michelle Chang, Friend of the Bride*
	Susan Hopkins, Cousin of the Bride
	Sharon Jackson, Friend of the Bride
Groomsmen	*David Hornsby, Brother of the Groom*
	Timothy Wilson, Friend of the Groom
	Raymond Cutter, Friend of the Groom
Flower Girl	*Rachel Hornsby, Niece of the Groom*
Ring Bearer	*Sean Hornsby, Nephew of the Groom*

The Nuptial Mass

Prelude
   Wedding Song   *Stookey*

Processional
   Jesu, Joy of Man's Desiring   *Bach*
   Canon in D   *Pachelbel*
   Trumpet Voluntary   *Clarke*

Greeting and Opening Prayer

Liturgy of the Word

First Reading
   Genesis 2:18–24   *Read by Samuel Alberts*
                                  Cousin of the Bride

Second Reading
   Colossians 3:12–17   *Read by Emily Simpson*
                                  Aunt of the Groom

Gospel
   John 15:12–16

Homily

Rite of Marriage

Declaration of Intentions and Consent

Blessing and Exchange of Rings

Lighting of the Unity Candle

Prayers of the Faithful   Read by Anne Lawrence
                                  Friend of the Bride

Liturgy of the Eucharist

Presentation of the Gifts   Thomas Williamston
                                  Allen Huang
                                      Friends of the Groom

Preparation of the Gifts
   Prayer of Saint Francis   _____ Temple
Communion
   Here I Am, Lord   Schutte
Presentation of Flowers
   to Virgin Mary
      Ave Maria   Schubert

Closing Rites

Final Blessing
Recessional
   Ode to Joy   Beethoven

Back Page

We would like to thank our families and
friends for their unconditional love
and constant support.
We are so grateful that each of you could
be here today to share in our special day.

❦

In this time of joy, we remember those
loved ones who are with us in our hearts.

Emily Jenkins, Grandmother of the Bride
Samuel Hornsby, Grandfather of the Groom

Getting to the Church on Time!

Before you can participate in your wedding ceremony, you have to get yourself and the rest of your crew to the ceremony site. Traditionally, it's up to the bride's family to provide transportation to the ceremony for the bride's attendants. Most often, this involves at least two cars or limousines: one for the bride and her father, and one or more for the mother of the bride and the bridesmaids. Often, these cars will leave from the bride's house or the bride's parents' home. (The bridesmaids are usually responsible for getting themselves to a designated meeting place on time.) You may also arrange for a car or limousine to pick up the groomsmen at a central location (the groom's house or his parents' house or the hotel where they are all staying) and drop them at the ceremony location. If that's not in your budget, the best man should help the groom ensure that every usher has transportation and will arrive at the ceremony at least one hour before it is scheduled to start.

Ceremony Seating Specifics

No doubt all of your guests will want to have a clear view of you walking down the aisle and reciting your vows, but it's your closest relatives who get the prime seats. Tradition has it that the bride's parents sit in the first row on the bride's side, and the groom's parents in the first row on the groom's side. The bride and groom's siblings and grandparents sit in the second row on each side. In some venues, the bridal party sits in the first row (in other cases, they have chairs to the side of the altar), which means everyone else is shifted back one row. The bride's parents and immediate family would then sit in the second row, and so on. Here are a few other guidelines to keep in mind when deciding where everyone will sit:

- In a Christian ceremony, the bride's "side" is on the left, as you are looking toward the altar. In a Jewish ceremony, the bride's side is on the right. Traditionally, guests are seated on either the bride's side or the groom's side, depending on who they know better.

- If the bride's (or groom's) parents are divorced, the bride's mother—and her husband, if she is remarried—sits in the first row, and the bride's father—and his wife, if he is remarried—sits in the third row. The second row is filled by close relatives such as grandparents and siblings.

Including Loved Ones in Your Ceremony

Have a special aunt you'd like to include in your wedding or a pal who didn't make it into the bridal party? There are plenty of other ways a loved one can participate in your wedding. Here are a few of the most common:

- A reading selection.

- Present the gifts at a Catholic ceremony

- Hold the huppah poles during a Jewish ceremony

- Light candles

- Sing

- Distribute ceremony programs

- A relative or family friend who is an officiant can perform the ceremony. (If the ceremony is to be performed at a house of worship with which your friend or relative is not associated, you will need to clear this with the officiant at that church or temple.)

- If the bride (or groom) is estranged from her mother and close to her father, then the father may sit in the first row and the mother in the third row.

- If one of the bride's (or groom's) parents is deceased, the other parent may have a relative or other companion sit in the first row with him or her.

- Special guests such as godparents are seated close to the front of the ceremony site, often in the fourth or fifth row.

- If you are having a military wedding, you need to take guests' rank into consideration when seating them. Check with your military representative for specific protocol guidelines.

After-Ceremony Etiquette

Several things are usually done right after the officiant pronounces you husband and wife—besides the kiss! One is the snapping of portraits of you, your new husband, and your families in the church or temple. If these pictures will only take a few minutes, you can do them while your guests are waiting outside for you to emerge. If they will take any longer, guests should be directed to leave for the reception so they don't have to wait around. In this case, you exit the ceremony location as though you're leaving (guests greet you, toss flower petals, etc.) but then reenter the church or temple after the guests depart.

Some couples form a receiving line after the ceremony. Others wait until they get to the reception to do the receiving line. The decision is up to you, based on your individual circumstances. For instance, if you have a large wedding, you may choose to wait until the reception. However, if you are unable to get into the reception facility right away, you may elect to do your receiving line in the time between the end of the ceremony and when guests leave for the reception.

Another post-ceremony tradition—and a great photo op—is the tossing of streamers, confetti, or rose petals at the couple as they emerge from the ceremony location. (Couples used to be showered with rice—a symbol of fertility—but that is no longer done since uncooked rice can be very slippery.) As the newlyweds leave the ceremony, guests gather outside to applaud and see them off as they climb into their cars for the reception. The car or cars for the bride and groom and the wedding party should be waiting at the curb in front of the church or temple. Some car services provide a champagne toast for the couples as they ride away as a new Mr. and Mrs.!

Can We Talk?

Q: My church forbids the throwing of rice, confetti, or rose petals. What else can guests do to give my new husband and me a festive welcome as we exit the church?

Annemarie, 25, New Jersey

A: It's understandable that you want a special way to mark your first few minutes as husband and wife. Some great options: Give guests pretty little bottles of bubbles and a bubble wand, small silver or gold bells to ring, or elegant streamers to wave. For those weddings where guests are allowed to toss petals or confetti, designate someone to clean up after your guests have departed or reimburse your house of worship for the cleanup expense.

Did You Know?

Many people have heard that tossing rice at the bride and groom is not a good idea because the uncooked rice is dangerous to birds who may eat it. That's just a myth, say the experts at the Cornell Lab of Ornithology.

Receiving Line How-Tos

- The bride's mother is the first person in the receiving line, followed by the bride's father, the mother of the groom, the father of the groom, the bride, the groom, the maid of honor, and the bridesmaids.

- Fathers of the bride and groom may stand in the receiving line, but they don't have to. But they should decide together—if one does, the other should.

- If the bride's (or groom's) parents are divorced, they do not stand side by side in the receiving line. The mothers can stand in the line, while the fathers circulate among the guests. Or, divorced parents can both stand in the line, separated by the groom's (or bride's) parents if they are still married.

- If the bride's mother and stepfather are hosting the wedding, they can stand together in the receiving line. If the bride's father is also remarried, he can stand in the receiving line with his wife—though the former spouses should be separated by the groom's parents.

- If the line is long (as in the case of a bride whose parents are both remarried), the bridesmaids needn't stand in the receiving line.

- If the bride or the groom have children from a previous relationship, the children can stand in the receiving line next to their parents.

- If the reception is hosted by someone other than the bride's parents (an aunt and uncle, for example), that person (or persons) are first in the receiving line.

- Greet each guest warmly and quickly to keep the line moving.

- Make your exchange with each guest sincere, but brief. Keep the line moving by introducing guests to the next person in line. For example, "Mrs. Smith. It's lovely to see you. Thank you for coming. Have you met my husband, Andrew, yet?"

- If you are wearing gloves (this goes for your mother and your groom's mother too) remove them before joining the receiving line. It is considered impolite to shake hands with gloves on.

- If you have your receiving line at the reception, have waiters circulate with food and drinks for the guests waiting on line to greet you.

- Ask for an empty table to be placed near the front of the receiving line so guests can put down napkins, glasses, etc. Neither you nor your guests should be holding food or drinks while you greet one another.

Make It Legal: Getting a Marriage License

Whether you choose a religious or nonreligious ceremony, your union isn't official without the document called a marriage license. The requirements for receiving a license vary by state and sometimes by county. To find out how to get your marriage license, check with the county clerk's office in the county in which you plan to marry or visit your state's website—many can provide the information you're looking for.

Here are some of the things you'll want to find out:

- Do we need an appointment to get our license or can we just show up during the specified hours?

- What forms of identification and proof of age do we need?

- What is the fee? Must it be paid in cash?

- Do we both need to apply in person?

- How long is the license valid?

- Is the license only valid in one particular county?

- Is there a waiting period? If so, how long?

- Is there a residency requirement?

- Is there an age requirement?

- Do we need blood tests or other medical information?

Things to Know About Marriage Licenses

- Some states have waiting periods between getting the license and when you can get married. In most cases, the waiting period is between twenty-four and seventy-two hours.

- Only four states—Connecticut, Mississippi, Montana, and Oklahoma—plus the District of Columbia still require blood tests for marriage.

- A few states have no age requirement, but most do. Check with your state for details.

- If you are divorced, bring your divorce decree with you when you apply for your license.

- If you are widowed, bring a death certificate with you when you apply.

- Most states charge a fee—usually anywhere from $15 to $65—and some require that you pay the fee in cash when you get your license.

- Most places require that both the bride and groom appear together in person to apply for the license.

- Be sure you have the documents you need. Some states accept photo IDs such as a driver's license, but others require a certified birth certificate.

Signed, Sealed, and Delivered

Once you get your marriage license, keep it in a safe place until you hand it over to your officiant. (Some officiants ask for it at the rehearsal—that will be one less thing you have to worry about on your wedding day.) The license will be signed by you, your groom, the officiant, and, in some states, witnesses (usually your honor attendants). Then your officiant will mail it to the license bureau and you can expect to get your certified certificate back by mail within a few weeks.

7

The Reception

Strike up the band (or the DJ), it's time for your social debut as husband and wife! Now that the more formal part of the day—the ceremony—is complete, you can breathe a sigh of relief ("We did it!") and get ready to party with your friends and family. From your grand entrance as newlyweds (when else will everyone you know rise and applaud as you enter a room!?) to the final notes of the last song, prepare to eat, drink, and celebrate. You've worked hard to get to this point, girl, so enjoy every minute of it!

The Right Reception for You

Wedding receptions can take many forms—from a casual brunch in a blooming garden to a sophisticated evening of dinner and dancing in a stately ballroom. And while the only two requirements for a wedding reception are cake and champagne, menus for celebrations today run the gamut. Ultimately, the time of your reception should dictate what is served. Here are some reception styles that are appropriate for each time of day.

IF YOU'RE HAVING	CONSIDER
An early morning ceremony	A breakfast or brunch reception
An afternoon ceremony	A light midday meal or an hors d'oeuvres and champagne reception
A late afternoon or evening ceremony	A full dinner and dancing reception
An evening ceremony starting at 8 P.M. or later	A cocktail reception with drinks and hors d'oeuvres or a decadent all-dessert party with specialty coffees and teas

Many guests assume that "reception" means dinner, though that is not necessarily true. If you're not serving a full meal, use words like "cake and champagne" or "cocktails and hors d'oeuvres" on your invitation to give guests an indication of what to expect.

If you are going to serve a complete dinner, you have two options: buffet or sit-down. Buffets, in which guests walk up to tables stocked with hot and cold dishes and select the foods they would like, are often less formal than sit-down dinners. The master of ceremonies can help things run smoothly and curb the formation of long lines at the buffet by calling tables to the buffet one or two at a time. A sit-down meal, which is usually more formal, means that guests remain seated while waiters and waitresses serve them each course at their table.

Did You Know?

There are several ways that a sit-down meal can be served. *Plated service* indicates that each guest will receive a plate with his full meal already on it. For *Russian service*, empty plates are at the table when guests sit down, and a server carries around a platter to distribute the food. Often, one server dishes out the meat or fish, another the vegetables, a third the rice or potatoes, and so on. *French service* denotes a setup similar to Russian except that servers work in pairs with one holding a platter while the other serves from it.

Creating a Crowd-Pleasing Menu

Designing a menu to satisfy a large group of guests can seem like a daunting task. But working with an experienced caterer can mean the difference between so-so food and real palate-pleasing fare. If your wedding venue has an in-house caterer, as many hotels, resorts, and clubs do, that will be the person with whom you'll work. Otherwise, you'll need to research and select an independent caterer. Seek out recommendations from people you trust, but be sure to choose your caterer based on her reputation for the type of food you want to offer. Just because you loved a particular caterer's Italian fare at your cousin's wedding doesn't mean you'll love her take on the Asian fusion dishes you desire for your reception.

Whether you go with an in-house cooking staff or an independent caterer, find out how the caterer handles guests with dietary restrictions. Ask if he or she can accommodate guests who keep kosher (some caterers have kosher kitchens; those who don't may be able to get a satisfactory meal from a kosher catering establishment) and what options are available for vegetarians (people who don't eat meat), vegans (people who don't eat any animal products, including eggs or dairy), and guests with food allergies.

If possible, schedule a tasting with your caterer. Some caterers will do a pre-contract tasting (before you book them) so you can test the quality of their cooking, but many, especially better known pros, will only do tastings once you have signed a contract. In this case, the point of the tasting is to choose your menu, not necessarily to determine if the caterer's cooking is up to par. When possible, limit the tasting to the key decision makers—you, your fiancé, and the parents, if they are paying for the reception meal. Just as too many cooks can spoil the broth, too many tasters can just confuse matters.

Finally, keep in mind that menus don't have to be dictated by the season (if you're a known ice-cream addict, go ahead and serve it for dessert—even in winter!), but you should work with your caterer to create a menu in which the courses complement each other. For example, a hearty first course such as a cream-based mushroom soup works well with a heavier entrée such as filet mignon. You wouldn't want to serve that soup with something on the sweet side like a citrus chicken. A chilled fruit soup, on the other hand, would be a perfect complement to the citrus chicken. The bottom line: Talk to your caterer—who's experienced in feeding large crowds—to come up with a menu your guests are likely to enjoy.

Can We Talk?

Q: Our budget doesn't allow us to host an open bar for our guests. Is it okay to have a cash bar?

Sharon, 22, Ohio

A: No! That's the equivalent of inviting guests to your home and then expecting them to pay for whatever they drink—and you would never do that. That said, you are not required to have a full open bar all night. Some budget-friendly alternatives include: having an open bar only during the cocktail hour and then serving just wine and beer for the rest of the evening. Or, skipping the open bar altogether and serving only wine and beer for the entire night. Finally, remember that you are not obligated to serve any alcohol at all—you can even substitute champagne with a non-alcoholic sparkling wine for toasting.

Savvy Seating

Figuring out guests' seating arrangements has gotten a reputation among brides as one of the most tedious parts of planning the wedding—and it really can be. In some ways, assigning each guest a seat is like putting together a jigsaw puzzle. The good news: There are ways to make this dreaded task go more smoothly. First, think about who each guest knows and who they might enjoy sitting with. If you don't know a guest well—say, a friend of your fiancé's parents—ask the person who knows her (in this case, your future mother- or father-in-law) for help. Arrange the seating plan so that groups of friends or relatives are seated together. For example, seat all of your college friends and their spouses or dates together and all of your fiancé's work colleagues together. What if you have a group of twelve good friends but your tables only seat eight? Divide the group evenly among two tables and fill in the remaining seats with other guests who have something in common (age, alma mater, etc.) with others at the table.

Avoid creating a hodgepodge table where you stick everyone you don't know what to do with. Also, steer clear of tables were everyone is a stranger to one another. Having just a few people who know each other and can make introductions and initiate conversation makes for a more enjoyable evening.

Kids' Table?

Should you seat your youngest guests with their parents or at an all-kids table? In this case, your decision should be based on the age of the children and how well you can expect them to behave if left alone. Very young children will do best with their parents, who can help them through the meal. Older kids often enjoy a specially decorated kids' table that is outfitted with kid-friendly activities (crayons and coloring books or small, seated games) and favors. If your budget allows, consider hiring a local teen to keep an eye on the kids' table. If not, situate the table near to where the parents will be seated so they can supervise.

Seating Singles

Should you seat solo guests at a table composed of other singles, or would they prefer to be mixed in with couples? This can be a tough call, so you have to make the decision on a case-by-case basis. An outgoing pal who is looking to meet new people may enjoy getting to know other singles. On the other hand, a single person may prefer to be seated with her friends—even though they are married or paired up. One thing to avoid: seating just one or two single people at a table full of couples.

Bright Idea

Regardless of how you seat your single guests, make a point of introducing them around. Maybe you'll be an honored guest at a wedding or two down the road!

Seating the Wedding Party

When it comes to seating the bridal party and your parents, traditional seating arrangements are still used, but some couples adapt these rules to better suit their circumstances. Here's a look at the traditions it's okay to break.

HEAD TABLE

Traditional Way: The bride and groom sit at a long, narrow table or a U-shaped table that may be raised up on a platform called a dais. The bride and groom are seated in the center of the table, with the groom on the bride's left and the best man on her right. The maid of honor sits on the groom's left, and other attendants alternate seats by male/female. (If the bridal party is small, spouses and dates of the bridal party may join the head table. Otherwise, they sit with the rest of the guests.)

Fresh Take: Some newlywed couples opt to skip the head table and sit alone at a "sweetheart" table for two. In that case, the bridal party members usually sit at their own table or at tables to the left and right of the bride and groom, often with their spouses and dates. Other couples choose to sit among their guests and don't have a head table at all.

PARENTS' TABLE

Traditional Way: The bride's and groom's parents sit together at a table of honor, which is located near the head table. The officiant and sometimes the grandparents are at this table as well.

Fresh Take: The bride's parents and the groom's parents each host a table of honored guests that can include the officiant, grandparents, and others like godparents. (Divorced parents should be seated at separate tables near the bride and groom's table. They can each host a table with their new partner—if they have one—and close family members and friends.)

Seating Do's and Don'ts

- **Do** avoid placing any guest tables too close to the kitchen door.

- **Don't** seat older guests at tables near the band, DJ, or loudspeakers.

- **Do** give the officiant a seat of honor by placing him at a table with either the bride's or groom's parents or grandparents.

Did You Know?

You don't need assigned seating if you're having a cocktail reception or dessert reception for which guests are dining on finger foods or other easy-to-eat bites. Assigned seating is only necessary for buffets and sit-down dinners.

- **Don't** divide the room into "his" and "hers." Stay away from placing tables of the bride's friends and family on one side of the room and the groom's on the other. Instead, mix the tables to create a friendlier atmosphere.

Reception Time Line

Chances are your wedding planner, on-site coordinator, or maître d' is well versed in wedding etiquette and will keep the party moving along. Still, it's helpful to know the order in which the major reception elements usually occur. The typical wedding reception lasts four hours. This time line shows how that time is usually spent.

First Hour

- Bride, groom, attendants, and family pose for wedding pictures (unless the photos were taken before the ceremony).
- The receiving line forms.
- Guests enjoy cocktails and hors d'oeuvres.

Second Hour

- Guests enter the main reception room and take their seats.
- The bride and groom, bridal party, and other honored guests are introduced.
- The officiant or another guest offers a blessing.
- The best man gives a toast. After he finishes, others— often the father of the bride or the maid of honor—can say a few words.
- The first course is served.

- The bride and groom share their first dance (this can also be done during the third hour).

- Some couples have their father-daughter and mother-son dances at this point. Others wait until the third hour.

Third Hour

- The bride and groom have their first dance together and other special dances, if they haven't already.

- The main course is served.

- Guests mingle and dance.

Fourth Hour

- Dancing continues.

- The cake cutting takes place.

- Dessert is served.

- The bride tosses her bouquet (optional).

- The groom tosses the garter (optional).

- Guests begin to depart.

The Cocktail Hour

As you probably know from being a wedding guest, receptions usually begin with a cocktail hour featuring food and drink. Offerings can vary from very light fare such as cheese and crackers to a more elaborate spread that includes passed hors d'oeuvres and hot and cold food stations where servers dole out heartier appetizers. These days, innovative couples are infusing their cocktail hours with cultural flavor by serving ethnic foods like dim sum, mini tacos, or sushi.

Can We Talk?

Q: My wedding ceremony is at 3 P.M., but my reception doesn't start until 6 P.M. What arrangements do I need to make for my guests during the "free time" between the ceremony and reception?

Allison, 32, California

A: If possible, you should arrange for a place for guests to gather and perhaps have a drink—possibly at a relative's or neighbor's house—in the time between the ceremony and reception. If there's no one who can host that interim get-together, ask a few friends or family members to spread the word that everyone will be meeting at a particular spot—the bar at the hotel where many guests are staying is one convenient place.

Some reception venues have a separate, smaller room where the bridal party can hold a private cocktail hour, if they choose. If not, the bride and groom and their attendants can join the rest of the guests at the main cocktail hour.

Even though many guests will choose to stand and move around during this time, provide some chairs so that guests can sit down, if they desire. This is especially important for elderly people or others who are uncomfortable standing for long periods.

Everyone in His Place

As the cocktail hour comes to an end, the maître d' or banquet manager will begin to direct guests to the main dining room. On their way, guests should pick up their table cards (also known as escort cards). These cards contain a guest's name and table assignment so that each person knows where to be seated. Here are a few helpful table card guidelines:

- Arrange the cards on a table in alphabetical order so guests can find theirs quickly.

- You can make the cards formal (Mr. and Mrs. Matthew Wilson) or informal (Aunt Theresa and Uncle Tom).

- Consider naming tables instead of numbering them for a unique twist. For example, instead of tables 1, 2, and 3, name them after flowers (Rose, Gardenia, and Lily) or places the two of you have traveled (Paris, Rome, Madrid).

- If you name tables, ask your reception staff to familiarize themselves with the location of each table so they can direct guests.

Did You Know?

At very formal weddings, guests are often assigned not just a table, but a particular seat at their table. In that case, a place card is located at each seat. The place card should be positioned above the plate and contain the guest's first and last name on both sides of the card—this facilitates introductions with guests seated across the table from each other.

Introducing the New Mr. and Mrs.!

Once all guests are seated at their tables, the master of ceremonies (often the DJ or bandleader) announces the entrances of the parents, the bridal party, and the bride and groom. Guests may remain seated or stand as the parents and bridal party enter, but they rise as the bride and groom are announced. Guests typically applaud the entrance of each of these special arrivals. In some cases, the bride and groom choose to be the only ones introduced into the room. If the whole group is to be announced, they enter in this order:

1. *Bride's parents*

2. *Groom's parents*

3. *Flower girl*

4. *Ring bearer*

5. *Bridesmaids and ushers (in pairs)*

6. *Best man and maid of honor*

Can We Talk?

Q: I'm keeping my maiden name. What should the bandleader say in place of "Mr. and Mrs." when he announces my husband and me at our reception?

Rachel, 27, Washington, DC

A: Simply tell your bandleader to say, "I would like to present, in their first appearance as husband and wife, Rachel Smith and Robert Jones."

The First Dance

When it's time for you and your new husband to take to the floor for your first dance, the master of ceremonies will announce it, and your chosen song will begin. Partway through the song, the emcee usually asks your parents, your husband's parents, and the bridal party to join you on the dance floor. The best man dances with the maid of honor while your bridesmaids and groomsmen pair up. A bridesmaid usually dances with the same groomsman she walked down the aisle with at the ceremony. If you have an uneven number of bridesmaids and groomsmen, a guest can step in—for example, if there are more women than men, a bridesmaid can dance with her spouse or fiancé—to even up the sides. Eventually, toward the end of the song, all guests may be invited onto the dance floor.

Bright Idea

Since all eyes will be on you and your man as you begin your first dance, why not take dance lessons before your wedding so you can wow the crowd with your fancy footwork? The waltz is traditional, but try tango or swing if one of those better reflects your personalities.

The Blessing

Before the meal is served, your officiant or another guest often says grace or other words of gratitude before everyone begins to eat. All guests, regardless of their religious affiliation, should remain silent and respectful while the blessing is given. Talk to your officiant or another guest well in advance about doing the blessing so they have time to prepare a few words.

Toasting the Newlyweds

Toasts are a traditional part of a wedding reception. They offer a way for your friends and family to wish you and your new husband health, happiness, and success in your new life together. The best man always gets the honor of giving the first toast. This is usually done either right before the main meal is served or immediately after. The best man and the guests will rise, and he will say a few words about the bride and groom and offer his best wishes. After the best man's toast, others may give their own toast. Often the father of the bride and/or the maid of honor will opt to speak. Many newlywed couples today also give their own toasts—to each other and to their family and friends to thank them for their love and support. This can be done after the other toasts are completed or at the end of the evening before guests begin to leave.

Toasts at the reception should be shorter and more formal than they were at the rehearsal dinner. Otherwise, the same toasting tips apply. See page 63 in chapter 4: "The Rehearsal Dinner," for advice on giving a great toast. And don't forget: When your friends and family are toasting you, don't stand or lift your glass; simply smile and thank the speaker.

The Father-Daughter Dance

At some point during the night—but always after your first dance with your new husband—it's customary to take a "farewell" twirl around the dance floor with your dad. How it works: The emcee will announce the father-daughter dance and your dad leads you out onto the floor to dance to a song that is special to the two of you.

If your father is deceased or estranged, you may dance with another male who is important to you such as a brother, uncle, or grandfather. Similarly, if you are closer with your stepfather than your birth father, you may choose to dance with him instead.

Mother-Son Dance

After you complete your special dance with your father or other escort, your husband can lead his mom out onto the floor to dance to a song that is significant for them. As with the bride, the groom may dance with another special woman (a stepmother, aunt, sister, grandmother) instead.

Did You Know?

At some point during the reception, you and your groom should each take a turn around the dance floor with your in-laws and with each other's honor attendants.

The Cake Cutting

When it gets to be about a half hour before the end of the reception, it's time to cut that sweet treat known as the wedding cake. While wedding cakes come in a variety of shapes (round layers *versus* square layers, for example) and flavors (white cake with white icing is no longer considered the only acceptable option), the procedure for cutting the cake is pretty standard: You hold the knife in your right hand, and your hubby places his right hand over yours. Together, you slice into the bottom layer of the cake. Your groom then feeds you a small piece of cake, you feed him a bite, and then you seal it with a kiss. The waitstaff will then bring the cake into the kitchen so it can be sliced and served to your guests. If you are having an additional dessert besides the wedding cake, that will be served now as well, along with coffee and tea. One tip: The cake cutting is often a signal that guests can leave—most will not leave before that—so don't do it too early or guests will head out before you want the party to end.

Bright Idea

Wedding cakes can be expensive! If cost is a concern, it's perfectly fine to use a small decorative cake for the cutting ceremony and supplement that with slices of sheet cake (they should be the same flavor as the decorative cake) that are in the kitchen. This also works well for large weddings since even a three- or four-tier cake might not yield enough slices for two hundred or more guests.

Did You Know?

Some wedding receptions feature two cakes: the bride's cake, or wedding cake, traditionally a towering white confection, and the groom's cake, traditionally a fruitcake. Groom's cakes are still popular today, but they are more likely to be made of chocolate or another non-fruit flavor. They are also generally decorated to represent the groom's hobby or interests—for instance, a cake shaped like a golf club or a sailboat. The groom's cake is displayed during the reception and may be sliced and served along with the wedding cake, or it can be given to guests in small take-home boxes to be enjoyed later.

The Bouquet Toss

During the last hour of the reception, it's customary for all single women guests to gather for the bride's bouquet toss. Legend has it that the woman who catches the bouquet will be the next to marry. The bouquet toss is optional—and some contemporary brides choose to skip it—but those who do the ceremonial toss typically use a special "throwaway" bouquet that their florist creates specifically for tossing. That way, the bride can preserve her actual bouquet.

Some brides opt against this ritual and choose instead to present their bouquet to a close female relative, such as her mother or grandmother, as a token of love and appreciation. Another option: the anniversary dance. The DJ or bandleader calls all married couples onto the dance floor for a slow song. He gradually narrows down the couples by asking those married less than a day (the bride and groom) to exit the dance floor, then those married less than one year, less than five years, and so on until only the longest married couple remains. The bride then presents that couple with a bouquet.

The Garter Toss

Like the bouquet toss, the garter toss is a tradition that is completely optional. If a couple chooses to do it, the groom will remove the garter from the bride's leg and throw it to a group of single men. Like the bouquet, legend says that the guy who catches the garter will be the next to marry. Sometimes the ritual will end with the man who catches the garter putting it on the leg of the woman who caught the bouquet.

Saying Good Night to Guests

Traditionally, the bride and groom made their exit from the reception (heading to their honeymoon) with a big send-off from their guests before the party ended. They would change into their traveling or going-away clothes and take off in a limousine or a car decorated with a "Just Married" sign. However, with so many guests traveling in from out of town these days, many brides and grooms remain at the reception until the very end to spend as much time as they can with their friends and relatives.

Can We Talk?

Q: What is a "Grand March"?

April, 23, Georgia

A: The Grand March is a popular ritual at many receptions. The newlywed couple, walking arm in arm, lead their guests around the room in a festive march. Then they form an arch by holding their arms up toward each other. The guests pass beneath the bride and groom's arms in pairs and hold up their arms to continue the arch. When all the guests have passed through the arch, the last couple (followed by the rest of the guests) passes back through again to kiss the bride and groom. Eventually, just the bride and groom are left and then they dance their final song before leaving the reception.

Wedding Favors

Some newlyweds choose to give their guests a small gift or memento by which to remember the wedding. It was once assumed that anything the bride and groom touched was lucky—so favors were a way of spreading that luck to their guests.

Favors aren't required, but if you do choose to have them it's best to give a small gift that is either edible (cookies with your initials on them in icing are adorable) or useful (small picture frames can always find a place on a desk or bedside table). What to avoid? Single items with the bride and groom's names inscribed. A solo wineglass with the words "Michael and Sally's Wedding," for example, is unlikely to get used. If you marry around a holiday, consider carrying that theme through with your favors. Christmas wedding? Give ornaments or red candles. Tying the knot in autumn? Present guests with yummy caramel apples.

Fabulous Favors

Jordan almonds wrapped in tulle are a traditional wedding favor, but these days couples are getting creative with the gifts they give their guests. Some hot options: edible items like candy and wine and "living" favors like herbs or saplings. Consider one of these guest-pleasing ideas:

¥ Wine with labels personalized with the bride and groom's names and wedding date

- To-go boxes to fill up at a dessert buffet, so guests can take home a treat

- Packages of flower seeds

- Small potted plants or herbs

- Custom music CDs featuring songs from the wedding

- Framed photographs or drawings

- Candy or cookies in a decorative box

- Candles

- Scratch-off lottery tickets

- Mugs with gourmet coffee beans

At the reception, the favors can be placed at each guest's seat or arranged prettily on a table near the door—that way, guests can take one as they leave. In lieu of take-home favors, some couples opt to make a charitable donation in each guest's name. In that case, it's nice to leave a small printed card (or a paper scroll) on each plate explaining that a donation has been made and naming the charity.

A Reception at Home

Home receptions can be charming and full of sentimental value, but they can also be tough to plan—especially if you're hosting a formal dinner and dancing celebration. If you have your heart set on a home-sweet-home affair, keep these tips in mind:

- Consider hiring a wedding planner to manage the myriad details associated with a home wedding, such as renting chairs, tables, linens, a dance floor, portable heaters or air-conditioning units, and so forth—things you might not have to arrange for if you were having your wedding in a hotel or catering hall.

- Be prepared for bad weather. A backyard ceremony and reception can be lovely, but have a backup plan in case Mother Nature is less than kind. You'll need to have enough room inside the house to accommodate all of your guests.

- Rearrange or temporarily move out some furniture in order to make more room for your guests to stand (or to fit folding chairs). Do this well in advance of the wedding.

- Rent portable restrooms if you are having a good-size crowd. Typically, a home's regular bathrooms aren't enough.

- Provide ample parking for your guests. Consider hiring a valet service.

- Ask a friend or your mother to greet guests at the door as they arrive and direct them to the ceremony and/or reception area.

- Give your neighbors a heads-up about the extra traffic you expect on the street that day. The last thing you need is an angry neighbor storming your party!

Taking Care of Your Vendors

Many of your professionals—from your event coordinator to your photographer and videographer—will be spending several hours at your wedding. Following you around with a camera all day doesn't leave much time for snacking, so arrange for your pros to eat at the reception. Many wedding professionals actually stipulate in their contracts that a meal must be provided, but even if yours don't, it's a goodwill gesture toward the people who are working hard to make your day special. You don't, however, need to serve your vendors the same fancy grilled sea bass or prime rib meal you're serving your guests. Talk to your caterer—many offer sandwiches and other low-fuss meals at a reduced price. Finally, provide them with beverages, but not alcohol.

8

Receiving Gifts

During the next few months you'll probably receive more presents than at any other time in your life. Your friends and family will be eager to help outfit your newlywed household, and if you're like most brides, you'll get more excited about nonstick cookware and kitchen appliances than you ever dreamed possible. To make gift selection easier for your guests and to ensure you don't get red bath towels when you have your heart set on those gorgeous sage ones (you know, the ones that match the fabulous shower curtain you found), consider registering your gift preferences. Afraid registering seems a little, well, greedy? Rest assured that most guests appreciate help from registries because they know they're getting something you really want. After all, no one wants to give a present the recipient will hate. Before you head to the mall to open your registry account, read

on for the specifics of registering, plus tips on tactfully handling a variety of gift situations.

How Registering Works

What exactly is a registry? It's a "wish list" of all the things you'd
love to have for your first home as Mr. and Mrs. During your
registry "shopping spree" (leave your wallets at home!), you
and your fiancé can pick out everything from housewares to furnishings to equipment for your favorite hobbies. The stores at
which you "shop" will maintain a list (the registry itself) of all
the items you would like to receive. That way, friends and family
have a ready-made set of items from which to choose a gift.
This can be especially helpful for guests who don't know you
well—business associates of your parents or future in-laws, for
example. Also, the stores where you register keep track of what's
been purchased for you, helping ensure that you don't end up
with three blenders but no toaster. Every time a guest buys something from your registry, the salesperson should update your
list electronically to indicate that a particular item has been purchased.

To make the best use of your registry, select items at a
variety of price levels. You'll want a good mix of stuff from
$125 china place settings to $5 place mats. That way, gift givers
can find something that fits their budget. Don't be afraid to
add a few big ticket items as well, such as a wine bar or vacuum
cleaner. Groups of friends or relatives may want to chip in on
a special purchase. Finally, choose a large number of items, especially if you are inviting a lot of people to your wedding. There's
nothing worse for a guest than finding that everything on a
couple's registry has already been purchased.

Who Can Register

Any engaged couple can register their gift preferences. Even if you've been married before, it's still appropriate to register this time around. If you have all the housewares you could ever use, consider registering for nontraditional items like luggage, gourmet cooking implements, gardening tools, electronics, or even camping equipment—whatever suits your fancy.

Timing It Right

If possible, register at least six months before your wedding. If you're having a shorter engagement, register as soon as possible. Even if you're crunched for time, try to start your registry prior to any pre-wedding events such as engagement parties, since guests may be looking for gift ideas. You can always go back and add to your registry before your bridal shower or wedding.

Did You Know?

No reference should be made to gifts on engagement party or wedding invitations. However, it is acceptable to mention where a couple is registered on shower invitations.

Choosing a Store

One of the biggest decisions you have to make is where to register. Should you go for the large national chains? The trendy neighborhood place with the unique furnishings you love? Both? Don't limit yourself to traditional housewares stores. These days, couples are registering for things like cameras, scuba gear, and golf clubs, so keep your store options open. When selecting stores, consider the following factors.

Service

Different couples need different types of assistance, so find a store with a level of service with which you are comfortable. Do you want an expert to help you match table linens to your china or explain the significance of thread count? Then consider a retailer with bridal consultants on staff who can spend time introducing you to the merchandise and guiding you through the registry process. More of a do-it-yourselfer? Then an on-staff bridal consultant isn't a must—a knowledgeable employee who can set up your registry account and get you going may be all you need.

Convenience

Guests are more likely to shop from your registry if it's at a store that is familiar and easily accessible. (Keep in mind that not everyone is Internet-savvy and comfortable shopping online—so some people will want to buy from a store they can go to in person.) If most everyone you and your fiancé know live in the same area, then a favorite local shop is a fine option. But if your family and friends are fanned out across the country, go with a national chain that has branches in lots of different places. Also, keep your own convenience in mind when selecting stores. You'll probably need to make several visits during your engagement to make your selections (which could take more than one trip) and update your registry (unless you do it online). After the wedding, you may want to return to exchange duplicates or damaged gifts or redeem gift certificates.

Merchandise

A typical bridal registry can include everything from linens to ladles to luggage. To cover all the bases, select a store—or a group of stores—that carries a wide variety of merchandise. Large department stores usually carry the widest assortment of goods. You might opt to register at a department store plus a smaller store that specializes in cookware, furnishings, home improvement equipment, or anything else of interest to you and your fiancé. Consider registering at two or three stores. Also, be sure that the products the store offers are good quality. While it's fine to choose some inexpensive, trendy items, you'll want to build a foundation of classic pieces that you'll be able to use for years to come.

Bright Idea

Get to know your stores' registry consultants. If you have a good rapport with them, they're more likely to call you when new products come out that they think you'll love or notify you if items you select become unavailable so you can substitute something else.

How to Register

Yes, you know how to shop, but that doesn't mean you know how to register. Registering, while a lot of fun, requires you to make many decisions and to stay organized. Follow these steps for registry success:

1. *Sit down with your fiancé and discuss your wants and needs.*

   Even if one or both of you has household items from your

current home, now is a good time to upgrade to new and better products. (It's also a good excuse to convince your honey to trade up from his college frat house décor!) Also, discuss your tastes to see where they mesh. Start a "style file" by ripping pictures of items and styles you like out of magazines and catalogs. Brainstorm together to come up with a list of the items you plan to register for and the stores you want to hit. You can do preliminary research by checking out a store's website.

2. Find out if your store(s) require an appointment to register. If so, schedule a time to sit down with the registry consultant. If no appointment is needed, you can go anytime, but plan to visit the store when it will be least crowded. Weekend mornings and afternoons tend to be busy, so consider a weekday night (and avoid days when there are big sales going on). Allot plenty of time—don't try to sandwich in registering between dinner at 6 P.M. and a movie at 8 P.M.

3. If working with a registry consultant, have her help you map out a plan of attack since large stores can be intimidating (there are just so many choices!). You can expect the consultant to give you a tour of the store, answer questions about the merchandise, and help you choose items that best suit your lifestyle.

4. Familiarize yourself with the registry equipment. Most stores lend couples handheld scanners to "zap" items they want to register for. How they work: You aim the scanner at a product's bar code and input the quantity you would like (for example, you could scan the bar code of a martini glass and hit "8" to indicate that you would like eight of those glasses). A store

Did You Know?

Scanner guns—a novelty just a few years ago—have become commonplace. The newest trend, according to registry experts, are unmanned registry kiosks. Instead of checking in with a registry consultant or store employee to start your registry account and obtain a scanner, you will be able to create your own registry account at a computer station and then insert your credit card (as a safeguard to ensure you return the scanner), pick up a scanner, and start shopping.

employee or bridal consultant can show you where to find the bar codes and how to work the scanner – a job most guys actually enjoy.

5. Get going! Tour the store and check out the goods. Don't be shy about picking up glasses and feeling sheets and towels. You want to be happy with your choices. Don't feel that you have to register for everything in one trip. Focus on a few categories (say, dinnerware, stemware, and flatware or sheets, towels, and shower curtains) each time out.

6. When you're finished with a registry session, return the scanner to the bridal consultant or salesperson. Ask her to print you a copy of your list so you can check for errors. It's not unusual for a slip of the hand to turn a request for eight martini glasses into a request for eighty-eight!

7. Update your list periodically. A store's offerings change seasonally, and a few of the items you registered for when you first got engaged may no longer be available by the time your

wedding comes around. Review your registry from time to time—you can do this online or at the store—and replace items that have been discontinued.

Online Registries: Why They're Great

Are you addicted to e-mail? Planning to bring your BlackBerry™ on your honeymoon? High-tech brides like you will love that many stores now make bridal registries accessible online. You'll be able to manage your inventory of wineglasses, pasta plates, and other must-haves 24/7, from practically anywhere. You can update your list when gifts are received (the store should note any purchases on your registry, but from time to time an item will slip past them), find out if items you've chosen become unavailable, and add stuff when you realize, "Oops, I forgot a can opener."

Online registries make gift-giving easier for your guests too. How? Even if the store at which you registered isn't right in someone's neighborhood, a guest can still shop there easily by logging on to the store's website. A few clicks of the mouse, and your present can be gift-wrapped and in the mail.

How Online Registries Work

Some stores allow you to handle the entire registry process— from opening your account to compiling your wish list—right from your home computer. In other cases, you'll set up your account and browse in the store and then just monitor and make changes to your registry online. Either way, you'll have a password, which ensures that only you and your fiancé can add or eliminate items from your registry. (Good news for you. Bad news for the mischievous groomsman who thought he could wreak havoc with your selections!)

Check your registry regularly. That way, you can spot items that become unavailable (they'll usually be marked this way on your online registry) and browse online or in the store to find a replacement.

A word of advice: Though it's possible to complete the registry process without ever stepping foot in the store, resist the temptation to go the online-only route. Hit the store in person at least once so you can really check out the wares and make sure you're happy with your choices. You may find, for example, that the glass pitcher that looked so nice on-screen is actually too small in person. It's better to find that out now, rather than when you unwrap it at your bridal shower!

Bright Idea

A drawback to online registry access: Because checking out your registry is as easy as a few clicks of the mouse, it's easy to keep close tabs on your list, and that can make it tough for your bridesmaids (or other friends) to surprise you with a bridal shower. Why? Seeing your blender, comforter, towels, and wine rack all marked "fulfilled" over the course of a few days is a sure sign that shower invitations have gone out. If you want to be surprised, consider agreeing on a "cut-off" date after which you promise not to browse through your registry online—even if you're really bored at work one day!

Wedding Gifts

When it comes to wedding gifts, sending them in advance of the wedding is the way to go since it gives the bride and groom

Did You Know?

Gift registries are meant to make shopping easier for your guests, but they aren't obligated to select a gift from the registry. Some guests will choose a gift on their own from another store because they feel it's a more personal gesture.

less to worry about on their wedding day. Gifts are usually sent to the bride's home or her parents' house. If the couple lives together, gifts can be shipped to their residence (you can indicate the address you prefer on your registry). Some guests will elect to bring their gift to the wedding reception. Prepare for this by talking to your reception site manager to see if a staff member can watch the gifts or if a locked closet or room can be used to store them. Monetary gifts, popular in some parts of the country, are usually given at the reception. Guests may hand you or your groom envelopes as you make your way around the room greeting people. Some brides carry a white purse or decorative bag for collecting their cards. Others set up a mailbox or similar drop-off place. Some guests may send gifts after the wedding, and conventional wisdom says that they have up to a year to do so. In this case, gifts should be sent to the newlyweds' home.

Displaying Gifts

Traditionally, in some regions such as the South, gifts were displayed before the wedding at the bride's parents' home for friends and relatives to admire. This custom isn't followed very often anymore, partly because fewer guests are sending their

Can We Talk?

Q: My fiancé and I have both lived on our own for several years and between us we have all the housewares we need. Is it okay to note on our wedding invitations that we would prefer to receive cash instead of gifts?

Julie, 29, Minnesota

A: This is a common question, but unfortunately the answer is no. Gifts should not be mentioned in any way on your wedding invitations. The best way to let guests know of your preference is through word of mouth. You can make your wish known to close friends or relatives and they can tell any guests who inquire. Since you already have the basic housewares, though, why not consider registering for some fun things or luxury items? That way, guests who choose to buy you a gift will still be getting you something you will enjoy.

wedding gift in advance of the wedding—more guests are opting to bring their gift to the reception instead. If you choose to display your gifts, these guidelines will be helpful:

- The gift display is usually set up in the bride's parents' home or the bride's home (if she doesn't live with her parents).

- Don't display gift cards alongside the gifts.

- Don't display checks or monetary gifts.

- Arrange the gifts so items of similar value are grouped together. Don't place inexpensive items such as kitchen utensils next to pricey gifts like sterling silver or fine china.

Damaged Gifts

A package arrives at your door, and you tear it open to find what would have been a beautiful crystal vase—if it weren't broken into a handful of pieces. What should you do? First, check the packaging to determine if the gift was shipped to you directly from the store (or ordered online or by catalog). If it was, simply contact the store for a free replacement. Do not notify the gift giver of the problem or mention it in your thank-you note.

If the gift was shipped by the giver herself, say, your Aunt Jane, check the packaging to see if the box was insured (look for an insurance stamp or sticker applied by the post office). If it was, then call Aunt Jane and politely explain that the gift arrived damaged. She can then contact the post office or shipping company for reimbursement (which she will most likely use to replace your gift). If there's no sign of insurance (and no chance of fixing the item yourself), you need to decide whether or not to tell the giver about the damage. In most cases, it's best not to say anything because the person will probably feel obligated to buy you another gift.

If the giver is someone who probably won't visit your home—say, a cousin or a friend of your mother—then definitely don't say anything. Simply write a gracious thank-you note without mentioning the damage. If the giver is your best friend or someone else who will be at your home often and will expect to see her gift on display, you may want to gently explain the situation—without implying that she replace the gift. What to say? Something along the lines of, "I am sorry to tell you that the beautiful platter you sent arrived damaged. But it was a lovely gift and we really appreciate the thought." That way she doesn't assume that not seeing the platter she so lovingly chose means you didn't like it enough to display it.

Duplicate Gifts

You love the state-of-the-art mixer that you received—but you definitely don't need (or have room for) two of them! Even if you register, duplicate gifts aren't unusual, but fortunately they're easy to deal with. If one or both of the items were purchased at the store where you registered (check the box and wrapping), it is perfectly acceptable to take one of them back. If they weren't purchased from your registry, but you can identify the store one of them came from based on the box or wrapping, you can try to return it to that store. (Some stores will only give you store credit, but at least you can pick out something else.) Either way, write the givers thank-you notes as you normally would—without mentioning the duplicate gifts. One final word of advice: Don't be too quick to return every duplicate. Some, such as extra sheets, towels, or glassware, can come in handy later if your "originals" get worn out or broken.

Unwanted Gifts

Maybe your taste is sleek and contemporary but a friend gives you a gift that would be perfectly at home with her country-style decor. Or perhaps you love vibrant colors but end up with a piece of pastel-colored pottery. With so many people trying to shop for you, there's a chance you'll receive at least one item that doesn't exactly suit your taste. It is acceptable to return a gift, as long as you feel certain that the giver won't find out. That means asking your pal where she bought the cow-themed kitchen canisters (or asking for the receipt) is off-limits! Most often, it's best just to be gracious and hold on to a gift even if it doesn't fit your needs or décor. Write a thank-you note expressing your appreciation—surely you can find one nice thing to say ("The canisters are so cheerful! You know I love to bake, and the canisters are perfect for storing supplies like flour and sugar."). If you know the gift giver is stopping by, make her feel special by displaying her gift. Once she leaves, it's sayonara to the cows until next time!

If the Wedding Is Postponed or Canceled

No one likes to think about it, but there are times when weddings get postponed or canceled. If you decide to call off your wedding, you must return all of the gifts you received within a few weeks of announcing the cancellation. Believe it or not, even personalized or monogrammed presents should go back to their givers. Include a handwritten note with each item thanking the giver and explaining that you're returning their gift because the wedding was called off.

If you must postpone your nuptials, there's no need to return the gifts you've received. Simply pack them away until your new wedding date. However, if several months go by and it becomes clear that the wedding isn't ultimately going to take place, the gifts should be returned to their givers.

Keeping Track of Your Gifts

With gifts arriving one after another, it can be tough to get a handle on who gave you what when. Your best bet: Use the chart below to record details of each gift you receive. (You can create one master list or photocopy the following chart to make separate lists for engagement, shower, and wedding gifts.)

Fill in the gift (i.e., "formal place setting" or "comforter"), the name of the person who gave it to you, the store where it was purchased (in case you need to make a return or exchange), a description of the gift (include a few words that will be helpful when writing the thank-you), and the date you sent the thank-you.

GIFT	GIVER	STORE	DATE RECEIVED	GIFT DESCRIPTION	DATE THANK-YOU NOTE SENT

Writing Thank-You Notes

As the engagement, shower, and wedding gifts come pouring in, writing thank-you notes can seem like a Herculean task. But here's something you'll be happy to hear: It used to be that the bride was responsible for writing all of the thank-you notes, but fortunately grooms are now getting in on the act—and it's only fair! While you should still pen all bridal shower thank-yous (unless you have a coed shower), your groom should do some of the engagement and wedding notes. A fair way to divide the task: You write the notes to your family and friends and he does the ones to his.

At a loss for words? Thank-you notes should be gracious and sincere, and include several elements:

- Mention the gift by name.
- Refer to how you'll use the gift.
- Express your appreciation.

For gifts of money, don't state the amount, but do mention the fact that it's a monetary gift, as well as how you plan to use it.

Bright Idea

Set up a thank-you note station stocked with stationery, stamps, a pen, your address book/list, and your gift record list. That way, you can knock out a couple of notes when you have a few spare minutes without wasting time gathering your supplies.

When to Send

Promptness counts when it comes to thanking friends and family for their generous gifts. You may have heard you have up to a year after your wedding to send out your thank-you notes, but that's not true (sorry!). Here's the real deal on turn-around times for your notes:

TYPE OF GIFT	SEND THE THANK-YOU NOTE
Engagement	Within 2–3 weeks of receiving the gift
Shower	Within 2–3 weeks of the shower
Wedding gifts sent before wedding date	ASAP, but definitely before the wedding
Wedding gifts given on wedding date	Within three months of the wedding
Wedding gifts received after wedding	Within 2–3 weeks of receiving the gift

Many couples like to include a wedding photo with their thank-you notes. This is a nice touch—as long as waiting for the pictures doesn't mean the thank-you notes go out too late. Find out if your photographer can have the pictures ready within a few weeks.

Sample Thank-You Notes

At a loss for words? Here are some succinct but sweet ways to convey your thanks.

Thank-You Note for a Specific Gift

Dear Aunt Carol and Uncle Ed,

Thank you very much for the china place setting! Jason and I will think of the two of you each time we use it, and hope that you will be our dinner guests sometime soon. We so appreciate your sharing our wedding day with us. It wouldn't have been the same without you!

Love,

Megan

Thank-You Note for a Monetary Gift

Dear Aunt Joan and Uncle Fred,

Thank you for your wonderfully generous wedding gift. Megan and I are saving for a house, and you have helped bring us closer to that goal. We'll be meeting with Realtors before we know it! We are so glad you were able to celebrate our wedding day with us.

Love,

Jason

Thank-You Note for an Unidentifiable Gift

You unwrap a box and pull out a...bowl? (well, not really) candle holder? (possibly) piece of modern art? (yeah, that must be

Tips for First-Class Thank-You Notes

Before putting pen to paper, check out these Do's and Don'ts:

Do write a few notes each day so they don't build up and overwhelm you.

Don't type thank-you notes. They should always be handwritten. (You can compose the note on your computer if that's easier, but once you have your thoughts together copy them on your stationery in your own handwriting.)

Do write wedding thank-yous on formal white or ivory stationery. (Engagement and shower notes can be written on decorative note cards.)

Don't use colored ink. Penning your notes in purple or silver to coordinate with your wedding colors may seem like a clever idea, but black or blue ink are the most appropriate choices.

Do hold off on using your married name until after the wedding. You should only use thank-you notes with your married name printed on them after the wedding. Before the wedding, you can use a note card with your maiden name or no name.

Don't forget to send thank-you notes to people who've helped you, like the friend who hosted a shower in your honor or the relative who handmade your veil or hosted out-of-town guests.

Do keep good records. Use the chart above to keep track of your gifts and thank-yous.

it!) Yikes! How can you write a thank-you note for a gift when you don't have a clue what it is? Try this:

Dear Mr. and Mrs. Stein,

Thank you for your thoughtful and generous gift. The colors are lovely, and it will have a special place in our new home. Robert and I are looking forward to seeing you on the Big Day!

Warmly,
Megan

Bright Idea

If your photographer is providing you with thank-you note cards with a slot for a photo, ask him to give you the cards in advance so you can write them out while waiting for your photos to be developed.

Did You Know?

A thank-you note really only comes from one person (in this case, you or your husband). Instead of signing your note "Love, Karen and Jake" mention your husband in the note (i.e., "Jake and I want to thank you for the beautiful linens") and sign the note just from yourself.

Can We Talk?

Q: Some of our wedding guests didn't give us a gift or card. I don't know if their gifts were lost or misplaced, or if they simply didn't give anything. Should I still send them thank-you notes?

Erin, 31, Pennsylvania

A: Yes, sending a thank-you note is definitely the correct thing to do. Even sans gift, every guest should receive a handwritten note expressing your gratitude to them for attending your wedding and sharing in your celebration. Don't forget: Wedding gifts, though customary, are not required. If the gift was lost or misplaced, sending a thank-you note may help you find that out. How? If you send a note that doesn't mention the gift specifically, the guest who gave it may ask if you were pleased with what they selected for you. In that case, you'll know that they did in fact give a gift. Either way, check with the manager at your reception site to make sure no cards or gifts were accidentally left behind.

9

Weekend Weddings

If your guest list looks like a national telephone directory with relatives from coast to coast and friends spanning the globe, you're not alone. Many couples these days are finding that their loved ones are so spread out geographically that asking them to hop on a plane, train, or automobile to come in for a one-day wedding is less than ideal. A better alternative: Swap the traditional single-day affair for an extended celebration featuring a weekend-long series of parties and activities. Yes, planning a single-day wedding can be enough work, but the extra effort that goes into a weekend gala will pay off in the form of wonderful memories of a mini-vacation with those you love. Bonus: You and your hubby-to-be won't be one of those married couples who say they spent months planning and their big day was over before they knew it!

Choosing a City and Site

A wedding weekend can take place in your hometown, your groom's hometown, your current home, base, or anywhere else you choose. When it comes to venues—say a country inn or a big city hotel—arrangements can vary from booking an entire small property to reserving a block of rooms at a large hotel or resort. Smaller settings like a bed and breakfast may not have enough rooms for everyone. In that case, you'll need to find additional lodging at another hotel. But before you put down that deposit, familiarize yourself with the area so you're up on the local restaurants, lodging options, and activities (obviously, if it's your hometown you already know it well!). If you're selecting a resort that has everything your guests could possibly need right on the grounds, the surrounding area may be less important. If not, be sure the town or city has ample hotel space, activities, and meal choices for your guests.

Never book accommodations sight unseen. Scope out a hotel's rooms and common areas to ensure that they are comfortable and pleasant. Nothing will get a guest's stay off to a worse start than arriving at a dingy hotel room. Also, find lodging in several price ranges so there's something for everyone on your guest list.

Finally, anticipate the needs of all your guests including children, the elderly, people with disabilities, and pregnant women. Consider these questions:

- Does the location provide wheelchair access?

- Are rooms air-conditioned?

- Are there activities for children?

- Is there transportation between event locations? (Sometimes having a golf cart on stand-by to ferry those who can't walk far works out well.)

Getting Your Guests Up to Speed

Once you've secured a location and reserved a date, it's time to start notifying your guests about your upcoming wedding. You'll want to start spreading the word with a save-the-date card or wedding newsletter at least six months prior to the wedding. That way, guests can hold the weekend (and arrange for time off from work, if necessary) and reserve their travel and accommodations.

Save-the-date card. A simple card—which can be handwritten for smaller weddings or printed by a professional or on your home computer for larger weddings—tells invitees just the basics: the date and location of your wedding, and that a formal invitation will follow. See chapter 3: "The Invitation" for more information on creating and sending save-the-date cards.

Wedding newsletter. Like a save-the-date card, a wedding newsletter alerts your guests to your upcoming nuptials. You can print your wedding newsletter and drop it in the mail or e-mail it to your guests. Besides the when and where, a newsletter also provides additional details such as:

WHAT TO SAY	HOW TO SAY IT
Hotel prices	Hotel rooms have been reserved at the Echo Lake Resort in Charleston, South Carolina, where the wedding will take place, as well as at the Quality Stay, 2 miles down the road. **Echo Lake Resort** Double rooms: $200/night For reservations, call 222-555-1234 • Please let the reservations clerk know you are with the Taylor/Smythe wedding.

WHAT TO SAY	HOW TO SAY IT
	The Quality Stay Double rooms: $99/night For reservations, call 222-555-4321 • Please let the reservations clerk know you are with the Taylor/Smythe wedding.
Activities	Bring your bathing suit and sneakers! The resort offers swimming, tennis, golf, biking, and horseback riding.
Weather/Attire	In addition to your wedding wear, be sure to pack clothing for a casual cocktail hour in the resort's lounge, a friends versus family softball game, and a barbecue/pool party.
Town/City Information	Charleston has many fun things for visitors to do such as touring historic homes, taking guided walking tours, strolling along the beautiful waterfront, and shopping along Market and King Streets.
Transportation	We will provide shuttle service between the airport and the resort for guests who are flying in. All planned events will take place on the grounds of the resort, but you might consider renting a car if you want to explore the city or surrounding area on your own.
Address of your Wedding Website (if you have one)	For more information and the latest news, check out our website: **www.samandsusanwedding.com**.

Kids or No Kids?

As with a one-day wedding, it is ultimately your decision whether or not to include children in the festivities. Bear in mind, though, that an adults-only wedding weekend requires guests to leave their children for several days—something many may be unwilling to do. If you decide that little ones are welcome at some, but not all of the weekend's events, then you should provide (and pick up the tab for) child care during the adult-only happenings.

Figuring Out Who Pays

One of the biggest questions couples have about wedding weekends is: Who pays for what? Here are some guidelines:

Travel and Hotel: Guests pay for their own travel and hotel costs (but it is thoughtful of you to reserve a block of rooms and try to negotiate a group rate). If money is a concern, try to arrange for a guest to stay at the home of a friend or relative who lives locally. If you can afford to, it's nice to provide accommodations for your bridal party, but it is not required.

Transportation: If many of your guests are flying in, some may rent cars, but it's still nice if you can arrange a ride or a carpool to and from the airport. If you invite guests to join you for a meal at a restaurant that isn't within walking distance of their lodging, then you should provide a van, a bus (or a trolley—for a fun twist!), or arrange a carpool to transport guests without their own cars. Also, don't forget to provide transportation to and from the wedding. (Provide detailed maps and directions to all activities for those with cars.)

Activities: If you invite your guests to join you or your groom in planned activities such as an afternoon of golfing or a concert, then you should pick up the tab.

Parties: In general, whoever hosts the party foots the bill. For example, if the groom's parents offer to throw a welcome luncheon on the day before the wedding, they'll make the arrangements and write the check. Other friends and relatives may volunteer to host events as well. These people may be willing to pick up the tab, but sometimes the bride and groom or their parents will instead.

Did You Know?

It's customary to give a thank-you gift to friends and family who helped pull off your wedding weekend. That includes those who hosted get-togethers, provided free lodging for out-of-town guests, and performed other tasks like making airport runs. Thoughtful options: A bottle of wine, a bouquet of flowers, or a lunch when you return from your honeymoon. And you should always send a thank-you note as well.

Keeping Everyone Organized

One of the trickiest parts of a weekend-long celebration is the logistics. You'll have guests coming and going at different times from different places so don't be surprised if you start to feel like an air traffic controller! To stay sane, follow these guidelines:

Before the Weekend

- Keep guests informed of happenings via a periodic newsletter or updates on your wedding website.

- Provide guests with a complete information packet via mail. This can be sent with the wedding invitation, but it's best to send a separate mailing once guests have accepted. The packet should include things like a schedule of events; transportation information; details about local activities and attractions; suggestions of appropriate attire; the name and number of a local contact person (this could be you, your parents, a trusted bridesmaid or friend); maps and directions.

- Have each person who is hosting a pre- or post-wedding event send out an invitation and an RSVP card (or, provide a phone number and e-mail address for replies on the invitation). These invitations can be sent either in your guests' wedding packet or separately.

- Create a master list of guest arrivals. Don't rely on your overtaxed memory—write everything down. This can help you coordinate transportation, if necessary.

- Keep a master list of transportation arrangements to ensure that everyone gets where they need to go.

During the Weekend

- You'll score major hostessing points by leaving a welcome basket (see chapter 10: "Destination Weddings" for ideas of what to include) and a schedule of the weekend's events in each guest's room.

- Provide each guest with information and schedules for local attractions and activities, as well as a list of some favorite restaurants. Say your wedding is in New York City. Arm guests with a subway map and brochures or schedules and prices for places like the Empire State Building, Statue of Liberty, and the Metropolitan Museum of Art. This can also be left in the guests' rooms ahead of their check-in.

- Keep your bridesmaids informed so they can help guests. Make sure they each have an updated schedule of event times and locations so they can direct wayward guests.

Appoint someone to be the point person for out-of-town guests. Choose someone who is knowledgeable about the area and a good problem-solver. Don't take on this task yourself as you'll be too busy finalizing details and visiting with your guests.

Did You Know?

If a friend or relative offers to host a gathering during your wedding weekend, you should provide her with a list of guests' names and addresses so she can send out invitations.

Appealing Event Ideas

Now that your guests have arrived, what are you going to do with them? If you need some inspiration when it comes to planning weekend events, check out these popular options.

The Day Before the Wedding

Welcome Party

Kick off the weekend with an afternoon picnic, dinner cruise, or wine and cheese party to break the ice among guests who don't know each other and set the tone for the weekend's revelry. This affair can take any form you choose, but a casual event that encourages mingling and introductions is best. Consider choosing a themed event such as a clambake for a New England wedding, a Chinatown meal for San Francisco visitors, or a country-western dinner and dancing if you're in Texas.

Rehearsal Dinner

The other big pre-wedding event is the rehearsal dinner. Typically, only immediate family and your attendants (and their spouses or dates) are invited to the rehearsal dinner. However, many couples who host a wedding weekend choose to extend the celebration to include all of their guests who have come in from out of town. If you prefer to keep your rehearsal dinner more intimate, you have two options. If all the key players (officiant, bridal party, parents) are available two nights before your wedding, have the rehearsal and the rehearsal dinner then—before out-of-towners start arriving. If that isn't feasible, you can still keep your rehearsal dinner small, but plan an alternate event for the guests who aren't included in the rehearsal. This would be a good time to take that family friend up on her offer to host a pre-wedding dinner or cocktail party. If no one has offered, you and your groom (or your parents) can plan and pay for an evening for your guests yourselves.

The Day of the Wedding

You might want to keep the following activities casual, since today's ceremony and reception will likely be more formal. Keep in mind that some guests may choose not to participate in a group activity, preferring instead to relax on their own.

- Light breakfast
- Softball game or golf outing (if the wedding starts later in the day)
- Picnic
- Sightseeing (organize a tour or guests can strike out on their own)
- Free time for swimming, hiking, tennis, etc., if available.

The Day After the Wedding

Farewell Brunch

Plan your good-bye brunch for late morning (around 10 or 11 A.M. is best) so that guests who like to sleep in won't miss it, and those who have to catch an afternoon flight have time to eat before they go. The food selection doesn't have to be fancy—chances are everyone ate and drank a lot at the reception the night before. A selection of fruit, baked goods, juices, coffees, and teas can work well.

Do's and Don'ts for the Bride and Groom

Some final weekend wedding tips:

Do get things organized before your guests arrive. If your wedding is in a city or town other than where you live, arrange to arrive a day or two before your guests. That way, you'll have time to take care of last-minute details like getting your nails done and meeting with your banquet manager a final time before everyone else gets there.

Don't wait until the last minute to book activities. If you want to treat your guests to a dinner cruise on a nearby river or a guided walking tour of the city, purchase tickets and/or make reservations well in advance. People will be disappointed if the promised activity is sold out when you arrive.

Do attend every event held during your wedding weekend. You don't have to stay the entire time (some guests may want to party all night, while you choose to get some sleep!), but you should make an appearance and spend a good deal of time with your guests.

Don't make events mandatory for your guests. Unlike the bride and groom, guests aren't obligated to attend every planned activity. Encourage people to participate, but let each person decide what and how much they want to do.

Do leave guests some free time. Avoid the "cruise director syndrome" where you aim to fill up every minute of your guests' day. A few carefully chosen activities are best.

Don't hesitate to introduce guests who don't know each other. Part of the charm of a weekend-long wedding is that your and your fiancé's friends and family have plenty of opportunities to get to know each other. Make guests feel welcome and included by introducing them to the rest of the crowd.

10

Destination Weddings

Does the idea of running off with your man to say your vows on a bluff overlooking crystal-clear tropical waters appeal to you? Do you want to follow in Madonna's footsteps and tie the knot at a centuries-old European castle? Or perhaps you're planning a second or third wedding and want to carve out some quality time for your newly combined family to bond away from the stresses of home. Whatever the reason, if the classic wedding-near-home scenario is a little too tame for your tastes, a destination wedding might be for you. Sound good? Then break out your passport and prepare for the trip of a lifetime!

Finding Your Dream Location

The biggest decision you face in planning an away wedding: Where to go? Even if you know, for example, that tropical "I do's" are for you, you still have a number of potential island hot spots to choose from. Do you want to hula in Hawaii? Salsa in Puerto Rico, or merengue in the Caribbean?

If you have a wedding destination in mind, but you've never visited the spot before, pick the brain of a knowledgeable travel agent or a wedding planner who is experienced in managing destination weddings. Their firsthand knowledge of individual islands, cities, and countries can be invaluable. They'll likely ask you lots of questions to help suss out which spot is best for you. Here are some things to consider:

- **Distance.** How far are you willing to go? If you live on the East Coast, the Bahamas might be a quick hop, whereas Kauai is a longer haul. Many European cities require six- to eight-hour flights from New York City— plus, don't forget to factor in the time differences (and the effects of jet lag).

- **Weather.** Research weather patterns in the places that interest you most—especially if you hope to have all or part of your wedding outside. Many people are surprised by how rainy Paris can be! If you're flexible on the time of year you marry, then you can book your favorite location when the weather is best. Late summer/early fall, for example, is hurricane season in parts of the Caribbean.

- **Accessibility for your guests.** You and your fiancé may be sturdy types who can go anywhere easily, but if you're inviting guests to your destination wedding, you need to keep their limitations in mind. A tropical rain forest accessible only on foot along a small path might be super-romantic, but it's probably not a good choice if you're expecting your eighty-year-old grandmother to attend!

- **Honeymoon spots.** Many couples spend their honeymoon on the same island or in the same city where they have their wedding, though they may move to another hotel or resort for privacy. Keep that in mind when choosing your wedding locale. Is this a town/resort you'd want to stay in for more than a few days?

- **Sentimental value.** The place where you and your soon-to-be husband first vacationed together or the city where you met may top your list of possible wedding locations.

Did You Know?

Getting married in another country can be tricky because each place has its own legal requirements. You can sidestep these concerns by wedding legally in a civil ceremony at home, either before or just after your trip. At your destination, you can still have a religious or spiritual ceremony and a reception.

- **Legal requirements.** Marriage requirements vary by country, so find out what's necessary before you book your wedding. Some countries have a residency requirement (the number of days you must spend there before your wedding); make sure you can meet it. You can find out the nitty-gritty on a location's requirements by checking with the consulate, embassy, or tourism board. Many popular wedding destinations provide this information on their tourism board website. Also, check to see if there are any language requirements (for example, the law may require that the wedding ceremony be done in the location's native tongue). If there are, you may need to hire a translator.

Booking a Site

Once you decide on a destination for your wedding, you'll need to choose a specific site or sites for your ceremony and reception. Many couples choose to hold both their ceremony and reception at the same place—often a hotel or resort. Others, however, opt to say their vows at one site—often a church or temple—and then have their reception at a hotel or restaurant nearby.

Where Should You Go?

Want to know where other couples are holding destination weddings? Here are the top ten places for marrying away, according to a recent *Bridal Guide* survey:

Florida

Hawaii

Las Vegas

Colorado

U.S. Virgin Islands

Aruba

Lake Tahoe

Jamaica

Cayman Islands

Fiji

The Internet is a great place to begin searching for suitable locations (and vendors, many of whom have their portfolios available online) in the destination of your choice. Start with the tourism board of the location you are interested in. There you should find listings of properties in the area. Many of the resorts and hotels you find will have their own comprehensive websites with pictures of the property, menu suggestions, and room rates. Once you've narrowed down your selections, it's wise to visit your destination (just a couple of days should do) and see the sites in person, if at all possible. You can also use that visit to interview vendors and finalize your picks.

Did You Know?

On some islands, there are public and private beaches. If you plan to have a beach ceremony and don't want strangers to be able to walk up and watch the festivities, check with the resort where you're holding your wedding to make sure their beach is private. Even hotels right on the water don't necessarily "own" that stretch of the beach.

When choosing a wedding site, look for a place that has experience in planning destination weddings. Many resorts and hotels have an in-house wedding coordinator who can assist you with most or all of the details—from flowers to cakes to marriage licenses. Some places even offer destination wedding packages that include wedding costs like flowers, a photographer, the officiant's fee, and more. These packages can make planning your wedding from afar much easier.

If you have your heart set on a place without an on-staff wedding coordinator, or you think you'll need additional planning help, consider hiring your own wedding coordinator. You can pick one who is based at your wedding location, or one in the United States who is experienced in planning destination weddings. Some wedding pros even specialize in planning weddings in particular cities or countries. You can find a destination wedding planner at Weddings Beautiful (**www.weddingsbeautiful.com**; 804-288-1220) or June Wedding, Inc. (**www.junewedding.com**; 415-279-7423) or by contacting the Association of Bridal Consultants (**www.bridalassn.com**; 860-335-0464).

Bright Idea

If you are meeting with vendors at your wedding destination, ask them to come to your hotel. That way, you won't waste precious time trying to find their offices in an unfamiliar city or town.

Inviting Guests

When you have an away wedding, your guest list will probably be much smaller than it would for nuptials near home. The reason: Destination weddings can be costly for guests, plus they require planning and travel, so you're likely to find that only your nearest and dearest will make the trip with you. Still, it is appropriate to send an invitation to anyone you would like to attend—don't nix them from your guest list just because you think they won't come. Send the invitation and leave the decision up to them. They just might surprise you! Alternatively, be understanding when guests decline your invitation. Some people may be unable to commit the time and money to attend a wedding far from home.

Save the Date!

To ensure the best turnout, you need to let potential guests know about your wedding as soon as you've lined up a place and a date. You can do this by sending out "save-the-date" cards—ideally, six months to a year before the wedding. That way, guests will have plenty of time to request vacation days from work and to make their travel arrangements. Save-the-date cards can be simple handwritten postcards or more elaborate printed missives. It's nice to match the card to the style of the wedding. For example, consider a colorful beach-inspired card for a wedding to be held oceanfront, or a card with a tartan plaid border if you're Scotland-bound. The card should have basic information such as when and where and let guests know that additional information will follow.

Here's a basic save-the-date card:

Save the Date!

Kara Simmons and Michael Frye are
getting married!

March 15, 2006

Paradise Island, The Bahamas

Formal Invitation and Details to Follow

Or, you can be more creative and include a poem:

Something Old,
Something New,
Save the Date
Or We'll Be Blue

✑

We're tying the knot
March 15, 2006
Paradise Island, The Bahamas

✑

Kara Simmons and Michael Frye

✑

Formal Invitation and Details to Follow

Sun,
Sand, and
Celebration!

❂

Save the date for

Kara Simmons and Michael Frye's
Hawaiian wedding

September 9, 2005

Formal invitation and details to follow

Follow Up

A few weeks after you send out the save-the-date cards, you'll want to follow up with phone calls to get an estimate of how many people are planning to attend. That way, you can continue with your arrangements—reserving a block of rooms at your chosen venue, inquiring about airfare, planning the menu, and more. Send out formal invites eight to ten weeks before the big day.

Who Pays for What

Like the rules for splitting the bill for any other type of wedding, the who-pays guidelines for destination weddings have evolved. Basically, what's "right" is what works best for everyone involved. If the bride's parents are willing to host and foot the bill, that's great. If not, the couple can pay or the costs can be divvied up among the couple, the bride's parents, and the groom's parents (if they're willing). Meals outside of the rehearsal dinner, reception, and other organized events fall into kind of a gray area—it's nice if the couple or their families can fund them, but most guests won't expect everything they do or eat to be prepaid for them. In general, here's how costs are often divided:

Hosts

- Pre- and post-wedding events such as breakfast or brunch the day after the wedding

- Rehearsal dinner

- Reception (food, drinks, flowers, etc.)

- Officiant

- Lodging for bridal party and sometimes guests (traditionally, the bride's family paid for her attendants' hotel and the groom's family for his attendants, but these days some attendants pay for their own lodging).

Guests

- Transportation
- Lodging (unless the bride and groom offer to pay)
- Meals and activities that aren't part of the planned group activities
- Incidentals

Special Considerations for Destination Weddings

Destination weddings offer plenty of benefits—picturesque locations, a days-long celebration for family and friends—but they also offer some unique planning challenges.

Here's how to handle common situations with finesse:

Choosing Your Bridal Party

Challenge: Selecting bridesmaids and groomsmen who are willing to travel.

Solution: When asking friends and relatives to be in your wedding party, let them know up front that you are planning a destination wedding. It's not fair to spring it on them ("By the way, we'll all be jetting off to Aruba!") once they've committed to being in the wedding. Also, if possible, you could offer to pick up the tab for their hotel stay to make being in your wedding less taxing on your pal's bank account.

Finding an Officiant

Challenge: Locating an officiant who is licensed to perform a wedding at your destination.

Solution: If you plan to fly in your own officiant from home, find out the requirements for getting him or her authorized to preside over your nuptials well in advance of the wedding date. It can be tricky—some places require that a foreign clergy member get a permit to "work" for one day. Or, ask your wedding coordinator or the tourism board for recommendations of local officiants.

Getting Gorgeous

Challenge: Renting formalwear at your destination and putting your hair and makeup into the hands of a stylist you've never worked with before.

Solution: Do your homework to determine if you'll be able to rent the clothing the men in your wedding party will need. If not, arrange for your fiancé, the best man, and other men to rent their clothing at home before they go. For a hair and makeup pro, again, recommendations are the way to go. Still, ask for a portfolio so you can see samples of their work. Also, bring pictures or magazine clippings of looks you'd like to show them.

Hiring Vendors

Challenge: Even if you visit your wedding spot in advance, chances are you won't have the time to interview numerous photographers, bakers, florists, and other pros.

Solution: Consider hiring a professional wedding planner to coordinate your event, or make use of the staff planner at your wedding location (most resorts and larger hotels have them). Use the vendors they have been happy with in the past. Also, you may be able to find good vendors through other vendors. Find a photographer you feel comfortable with? Ask him who is the most popular florist or hairstylist in town. Don't forget that the Web can be a terrific resource. Wedding websites such as **www.bridalguide.com** often have message boards where you might be able to "meet" brides who recently married at your location. Chat them up to find out which vendors they loved. Still, it's smart to try to assess your pro's talent yourself, if possible. It may be tough to check references in a foreign country, but you can ask for photos of a vendor's work or check out his website to see samples.

Selecting a Menu

Challenge: Some food and beverage choices may be unfamiliar to you.

Solution: Destination weddings offer a unique opportunity to introduce local cuisine to your guests. Research some of the foods and drinks that are unique to your environment (for example, if marrying in Bermuda, consider serving the island's traditional Dark and Stormy rum cocktail). It's also wise to have one classic dish on hand for guests who have dietary restrictions or are nervous about trying the local specialties.

Did You Know?

Many resorts and airlines offer discounts to groups traveling for a wedding. Check with individual airline carriers and properties to determine if you can get a reduced rate for your guests. No doubt your friends and family will appreciate the savings!

Taking Care of Your Guests

The fact that your guests are willing to pack their bags and follow you to your destination of choice shows how much they care about you. You, the ever gracious hostess, can show your appreciation by making their trip as stress-free as possible with these do's and don'ts.

Do some of the travel legwork for your guests. It's helpful to do some of the preliminary research and let guests know what airlines fly to your location, where accommodations are available, what the costs may be, and so forth. You should also reserve a block of hotel rooms for your guests (ask for a group discount) and check in with the airline about deals.

Don't become everyone's personal travel agent. Aunt Sally only sits in aisle seats? Cousin Gerry can't fly out before noon on Thursday? Although it's thoughtful of you to provide general travel information, don't get too intimately involved in your guests' arrangements. As the blushing bride, you already have enough to worry about. Instead, point them in the direction of a reputable travel agent for help.

Do appoint someone as group leader. Once you get to your wedding locale, you'll have plenty to focus on between finalizing the ceremony and reception details and getting some pre-wedding R&R. Recruit a willing and able friend or parent to act as a representative for your guests. That person can help solve guests' problems should they arise.

Don't keep guests in the dark. Provide your friends and family with plenty of detailed information about travel, accommodations, activities, restaurants, local transportation, and not-to-be-missed tourist spots—it'll generate excitement for the trip and energize your event.

If you—or someone you know—is Internet savvy, set up a website and post all of this information. You can also leave brochures, transportation schedules, and info packets in each guest's hotel room.

Do schedule activities for your guests besides the ceremony and reception. Give your guests a chance to explore their surroundings and spend more time with you and your groom by planning outings or activities everyone will enjoy. A sunset sail, a visit to that famous museum, a wine-tasting class, or another unique must-do at your location are all fun ideas. Also, include all guests in your rehearsal dinner, or plan an alternate event at the same time for the guests not invited to the rehearsal dinner.

Gift Basket Goodies

Your friends and family will rave about your hospitality if you surprise them with a welcome-to-my-wedding gift. You don't have to spend a fortune, just pick items that relate to the theme and location of your nuptials. Check out these ideas of what to include in a guest gift basket or bag.

Good for Anyone

- A welcome note from you and your fiancé
- Bottled water
- Small packages of snacks
- Disposable cameras
- Bath products
- Breath mints

Tropical Hotspots

- Flower leis
- Sunscreen
- Flip-flops
- Beach totes
- Beach towels

City Slickers

- Guide maps
- Card for the subway/underground
- Brochures about museums and other attractions
- A city-themed snack—croissants in France, scones in England, maple syrup in Vermont, and so on
- Mini photo album
- Language phrase book

Don't get insulted if guests forgo group activities. Yes, it's your wedding, but it's also their vacation so give guests leeway to strike out on their own as well.

Do have a welcome gift waiting in each guest's room. Show your guests how much you appreciate their presence by greeting them with a small gift. They'll be especially grateful if the gift includes something they may have forgotten to pack (say sunscreen or a disposable camera). For guest gift suggestions, read on.

Create a Wedding Website

A custom website dedicated to your nuptials can be a great tool for keeping your guests up to date on travel arrangements as well as providing them with plenty of details about your location. Add a few pictures of your destination, and your guests will be so excited, they'll be counting the days till departure.

If you—or a friend—are technically savvy, you can build your own website to your own specifications. If you're a little less knowledgeable, a number of wedding information websites let you create your own personalized pages free (**www.weddingchannel.com**), or for a small fee. Simply input your information into the template provided, and you're all set.

Don't forget to include these items on your site:

- Date and time of wedding

- Information about transportation

- Details about accommodations (put in links to the hotel or resort where you'll be having the wedding so guests can take a firsthand look)

- Listing of local attractions

- Photos of the island, city, etc., as well as pictures of the wedding venue and lodging

- General weather information

- Current exchange rate

- Notes on appropriate attire

- Details about other planned events and activities

What to Wear

It's your day and what to wear is certainly up to you, but you should consider choosing a style of dress that complements your wedding vibe. A full-skirted taffeta ball gown and opera-length gloves will look out of place on a beach (not to mention how hot and uncomfortable you'll feel). If you're marrying in another country, keep in mind the local customs. For instance, many places of worship frown on too-revealing dresses and some require shoulders to be covered. These guidelines can help you decide what to wear:

	Consider Wearing	*You May Want to Skip*
Beach	A sheath or slip dress or strapless gown in a breezy fabric such as chiffon or organza; for an ultra-casual wedding, a bathing suit and sarong.	Heavy fabrics like taffeta that will weigh you down, high heels, a long train.
Ancient Cathedral	A traditional gown	A revealing dress—you don't have to rule out a strapless or spaghetti strap dress, but add a wrap or cover-up to make it more modest
Mountaintop at a Ski Resort	A silk-sateen dress with a matching wrap or jacket. Great accessories: a fur hat, muff, or stole.	Anything too thin or revealing

	Consider Wearing	You May Want to Skip
Cruise Ship	If your wedding will be held indoors in a climate-controlled room, then pretty much anything goes—from a fairy-tale princess gown to a simple sheath or a dress with some tropical inspired color.	A veil or headpiece that isn't firmly attached to your head, if you're going to be ouside for a while. It can get pretty windy on deck.

Can We Talk?

Q: How can I politely let guests know that I'd prefer them to give cash instead of gifts for my wedding? I don't want to be stuck lugging boxes home from Jamaica.

Amy, 33, Wisconsin

A: True, toting presents home from your trip can be kind of a pain, but there's no socially correct way to tell guests what type of gifts to give you. It's a no-no to mention money or to indicate anything about presents on your wedding invitation. That said, if you let your parents or close friends know your preference, they can spread the word—but only if guests ask. Also, keep in mind that many guests won't want to schlep a box or package on the plane either, so they may go the cash/check route anyway. One final word: Don't be surprised if guests give smaller presents or no present at all. After all, they are likely spending a good deal of money to be with you on your special day and they may consider that their gift.

Working with Wedding Professionals in Foreign Countries

Like working with any wedding professional, working well with those in your wedding destination means good communication and respect. Other ways to keep your international relations friendly:

- **Be respectful of the country's traditions.** Remember that cultural differences such as how food is prepared and what constitutes a wedding ceremony are part of the reason you're choosing to tie the knot abroad. Don't expect people in other countries to succumb to the American way of doing things.

- **Be patient.** The rest of the world doesn't share our hurry-up attitude, so things can move much more slowly in foreign lands. Arrive an extra day or two in advance in order to accommodate the slower pace.

- **Let it go.** Consider yourself warned, darling: Destination weddings, by nature, aren't for control freaks. Remind yourself to go with the flow and enjoy the experience rather than obsessing over minor details like the color of table linens or the shade of pink of your flowers.

Wedding Announcements

Share the news of your far-flung nuptials with those who weren't at your wedding by sending out printed wedding announcements (don't send the announcements to people who were invited but declined; they already know about your marriage). The announcements, which can be printed on a card stock similar to your invitations, should be ordered from a printer in advance of the wedding. That way, you can mail them out either right before you leave for your wedding or right after you return. For more details on wedding announcements and the right wording for yours, see chapter 3: "Invitation and Wedding Announcements."

Post-Wedding Receptions at Home

Many couples who have an intimate destination wedding decide to throw a larger reception when they return home so that they can celebrate with the family and friends who couldn't make it (or weren't invited) to the wedding.

This reception can be as formal or as casual as you would like. You can plan a buffet or sit-down dinner at a favorite restaurant, a cocktail party at a hip hotel, or an all-dessert soiree at home. Follow the etiquette guidelines you would if this reception were your only wedding celebration. One addition: Don't forget to bring along plenty of photos or even a video from your destination wedding to share with your guests. Some couples even create slide shows of their wedding pictures so guests can see what it was like to be there. This is probably the one time your friends and relatives won't flinch at seeing your vacation pictures, so take advantage of the moment!

≈ 11 ≈

Second Weddings

Tying the knot for the second or third (or more!) time? You probably have a lot of questions. After all, some of the most pervasive wedding-related etiquette myths surround remarriages (Don't wear white! Don't plan a big reception!). The good news: The rigid rules of the past have relaxed as encore marriages have become more and more common. And since previously married brides and grooms tend to be a little older and more experienced than first-timers, you probably have a better idea of what you want in a wedding. So start daydreaming about the wedding of your choice, because this celebration should be one you'll look back on fondly for years to come.

Announcing Your Engagement

He popped the question. You said yes. Or maybe it was the other way around! Either way, you're ready to share the good news. If you or your fiancé have children from previous relationships, they should be the first to learn of your engagement. It's best to tell your children alone, rather than with your fiancé present. That way they have time to digest the news and to ask you questions. Plus, if your children's initial reaction is negative, you'll spare your future spouse's feelings by not having him present. Once your kids have had some time to get used to the idea, arrange a time for you, your fiancé, your kids and his to get together and talk.

After you've told your children, you can tell your parents and immediate family, and then your friends. You should also inform your former spouse. Even if you don't have children together, it's polite to tell him yourself, rather than letting him hear the news through the grapevine. A phone call or note is best. E-mail is acceptable only if absolutely necessary.

Newspaper Announcements

Whether or not to announce your engagement in the newspaper is up to you. If you were widowed or divorced recently, it is preferable to skip the engagement announcement and just publish a wedding announcement when the time comes. Never publish an engagement announcement if you are still legally married to someone else (even if a divorce is pending).

If you do decide to print an announcement, here is the correct format. If the name you are currently known by is your ex-husband's name, that is the name you should use in your announcement.

Mr. and Mrs. Kenneth Johnson announce the engagement of their daughter, Suzanne Johnson Harvey [or Suzanne Harvey], to Scott Thompson, son of Mr. and Mrs. Robert Thompson of Albuquerque, New Mexico.

What's Your Wedding Style?

One of the most important decisions you'll make is what you want the tone of your wedding to be. Are you looking for a big, roaring party? Or would you prefer a smaller, more intimate affair? You may even find yourself influenced by the wedding you or your fiancé had—or didn't have—the first time around. Maybe you've already had the huge traditional celebration, and now you'd rather do something simpler. Or perhaps you eloped or had a low-key event before and now is your chance to pull off the wedding of your dreams. The bottom line: There are no

Can We Talk?

Q: My fiancé and I have both been married before. Is it appropriate for us to have an engagement party this time around?

Dorothy, 36, Pennsylvania

A: Yes, engagement parties for second weddings are perfectly acceptable. There's no reason not to celebrate this engagement with as much joy as you would a first engagement. Since couples who are remarrying tend to be older and more independent than first-time brides and grooms, many choose to throw (and pay for) their own engagement party. However, if your parents or your fiancé's parents want to host an engagement soiree, that is fine too.

hard-and-fast rules about size or style for repeat weddings. In general, second or third weddings tend to be more intimate, but that's not a requirement. You can certainly opt for a quiet celebration, but don't fall for the misconception that that's your only option.

You'll also need to determine where your ceremony will take place. Depending on the laws of your religion, you may or may not be able to marry a second time in a house of worship. Speak to your clergy member about your specific situation. Civil and nonsectarian ceremonies are popular for remarriages because they give a couple more leeway to tailor the ceremony to their individual needs and preferences. See chapter 6: "The Ceremony" for more specifics on designing your nuptials.

Selecting a Bridal Party

When it comes to a second wedding, selecting a bridal party is no different than it would be for a first wedding: Simply ask the people you feel closest to to be your attendants. That said, some encore couples choose to keep their wedding party small, but the choice is yours. If you or your future husband have children, it's nice to include them in your bridal party.

It's also fine if your bridal party includes the same people who acted as your attendants at your first wedding. If they are still your closest companions, then there's no reason not to include them in this happy occasion.

Shower or No Shower?

Many people wonder whether it's socially correct to throw a shower when the bride and/or groom have been married before. The answer is yes. If you've never been married but your fiancé has, your bridal shower should follow the same protocol as it would for any other first-time bride. (See chapter 2: "Pre-Wedding Parties" for more shower information.)

Showers for second-time brides are still perfectly acceptable, but they are usually kept to a smaller scale. It's fine for your shower host to invite your close friends and relatives who may have attended your first bridal shower, but she should try not to invite too many people who showered you the first time around. If you've made new friends since your last shower, it's appropriate to invite them. Another alternative: Your shower hostess can plan an intimate luncheon without gifts if you are uncomfortable with the idea of a second shower.

Did You Know?

Registering for gifts when you remarry is not a faux pas, as some people believe. Some friends and family will choose to get you a present and it's helpful to them to know what you would like. If you already have the requisite dishes and linens, register for fun items like camping gear, a cappuccino machine, or a set of luggage.

Drawing Up a Guest List

There are no rules about the size of the guest list for second or more weddings. Whatever is comfortable for you is what's best. When it comes to people who may be, well, less than enthusiastic, about your upcoming nuptials, use your judgment as to whether they make the cut or not. One tricky set of potential guests is your (or your fiancé's) former in-laws. The general rule: If you are close with them (which is often the case when you have children—they're the kids' grandparents) and your future husband is comfortable with the idea, then you can invite them. Other than that, the guest-list guidelines that apply to a first wedding apply to your wedding as well. Chapter 3: "Invitations and Wedding Announcements" has the lowdown on who to invite and how to do it with style.

Can We Talk?

Q: I'm on pretty good terms with my ex-husband. Should I invite him to my wedding?

Amy, 30, Connecticut

A: Even if you and your former spouse have an extremely amicable relationship, it's still not appropriate to invite him to your wedding. There are several reasons for this: If you have children, they may be confused by their dad's presence at your wedding. And even if you and your ex are comfortable with his presence being at your wedding, other guests may not be, and that will put their focus on him instead of on you and your new husband. Finally, your former husband may not want to see you tie the knot, and by inviting him you're putting him in the uncomfortable position of having to decline.

Issuing Invitations

How do you word the invitation to an encore wedding? If you're hosting the wedding yourselves, the invitation comes from you; however, some young second-time brides prefer to have their parents issue the invitation (especially if the parents are footing the bill).

Mr. and Mrs. Jonathan Henry Wilson

request the honour of your presence

at the marriage of their daughter

Sarah Wilson [maiden
name] Taylor [first married name]

to

Marc Andrew Holmes

Saturday, the ninth of September

Two thousand and six

at half after three o'clock

St. Thomas Church

Springfield, Massachusetts

Mr. and Mrs. Jonathan Henry Wilson

request the pleasure of your company

at the marriage of their daughter

Sarah Wilson [maiden
name] Taylor [first married name]

to
Marc Andrew Holmes

Saturday, the ninth of September
two thousand and six
at half after six o'clock

The Asian Art Museum
San Francisco, California

The pleasure of your company

is requested at the marriage of

Sarah Wilson Taylor

to

Marc Andrew Holmes

Saturday, the ninth of September

Two thousand and six

at half after six o'clock

The Asian Art Museum

San Francisco, California

Sarah Wilson Taylor

and

Marc Andrew Holmes

request the honour of your presence

at their marriage

Saturday, the ninth of September

Two thousand and six

at half after three o'clock

St. Thomas Church

Springfield, Massachusetts

Can We Talk?

Q: My fiancé and I have all of the china, towels, and sheets we need. In fact, we just want our friends and family to share our wedding with us—and not feel obligated to bring us gifts. Is it okay to write "no gifts please" on our wedding invitations?

Barbara, 43, Kansas

A: While your intention is good, printing "no gifts please" on your invitation would still be breaking the cardinal rule of wedding invitations: Make no mention of gifts. Your best bet: Inform your closest friends and family members of your no-gift wish and let them spread the news via word-of-mouth. Even then, though, some guests may choose to celebrate your new marriage with a gift, so accept it graciously and enjoy!

What to Wear

Think you have to wear a modest, pastel-colored suit if this isn't your first walk down the aisle? Think again. That "rule" is completely outdated. Today's brides have many more attire options, including:

- A traditional white or ivory wedding gown
- A special occasion dress
- A suit
- A cocktail dress
- A flowing pantsuit

Even though a train and veil are considered symbols of virginity, many second-time brides prefer wearing a veiled headpiece or a gown with a train. Other accessory options include a tiara, hat, simple headpiece, or fresh flowers. If you do choose to wear a veil, don't wear the blusher (the section of the veil that covers your face). Blushers are better suited for very young and first-time brides.

Your groom also has a number of clothing options, and should select the one that best fits the formality of your wedding. Choices for guys include:

- A tuxedo
- A suit
- Pants and a blazer

Finally, if you have attendants, their attire should conform with the style and formality of the wedding. Keep in mind, if your bridesmaids are older, that they might not want to wear the traditional matching dresses. Consider letting them select their own dress within predefined guidelines (for example, tell them the color and fabric you would like and let them decide on the style).

Kid-Friendly Celebrations

If you or your fiancé have children from a previous marriage, you should definitely try to include them in your wedding day by giving them special roles and involving them in the planning process. Your goal: Make the children feel like an important part of the new family that is being created. Keep these guidelines in mind:

- Discuss your remarriage with your ex-spouse, so the two of you can explain to your children that it's not disloyal of them to be excited about the upcoming wedding.

- Don't push children who don't want to take part in the wedding. Though you should try to include them, if your child (or your fiancé's) doesn't want to participate in the wedding, don't force the issue.

- Find age-appropriate roles for each child. A young child can act as a flower girl or ring bearer while a school-age child could be a junior bridesmaid or junior usher. Older kids can be bridesmaids, ushers, the maid of honor, or best man.

- Consider including your children in the ceremony by inviting them to help you light candles or by presenting them with a symbol of your new family (perhaps a piece of jewelry or a medallion).

Wedding Customs and Traditions

Many brides wonder if they can include the same wedding traditions the second (or more) time around that they did on their first trip down the aisle. The answer: Yes, with some modifications that reflect your current family circumstances. Here's a look at common traditions, how they usually work the first time around (your "premiere") and how you can modify them for your new nuptials (your "encore").

	Premiere	Encore
Walking Down the Aisle	The bride's father escorts her down the aisle and often "gives her away" when they reach the alter.	The bride and groom may choose to walk down the aisle together or the bride may be escorted by a child from her previous marriage. The father of the bride can, again, escort her down the aisle, though he shouldn't "give her away." (You can avoid the "giving away" part by asking your officiant not to say "Who gives this woman in marriage?") Some couples skip the processional altogether and enter the ceremony from a side door.
Lighting of the Unity Candle	The bride and groom use the flame from their individual candles to light a shared candle.	If the bride and groom have children from previous relationships, the kids can help their parents light a family unity candle.
Selecting Readings	The bride and groom choose traditional scripture readings, often from selections preapproved by their officiant.	The bride and groom can select readings that are personally meaningful or that focus on starting a new life together.

	Premiere	Encore
Exchanging Vows	Couples recite traditional vows or write their own.	Couples write their own vows that include their children and new family. Some couples make vows to their children as well.
Receiving Line	The newlyweds often stand in the receiving line with their parents (who are often the hosts).	If the couple is hosting the wedding, there's no need for their parents to stand in the receiving line. Instead, many couples invite their children to stand with them while they greet guests.
Seating Arrangements	The bride and groom sit at a head table with their bridal party or at a sweetheart table by themselves.	The couple sits at a family table with their children.
The Honeymoon	The newlyweds head off for a vacation for two.	Remarried couples should still take a honeymoon—even if they can only get away for a few days. Some couples plan a two-part trip: one part for the two of them and a second part that includes their children.

Did You Know?

Guests are not obligated to give you a wedding gift, particularly if they gave you one for your first marriage. Still, many friends and family will choose to mark this new milestone with a present to you and your new husband.

Wedding Announcements

Once you're officially married, it's time to send out wedding announcements—if you choose to use them. Strictly speaking, wedding announcements should be in the mail within twenty-four hours of your marriage ceremony, but up to several months after your wedding is acceptable.

Wedding announcements can be issued by you or your parents. Older couples and those who hosted their own weddings may wish to issue their own announcements. Here are three common wording options:

> *Mr. and Mrs. Joseph Anderson*
> *have the honour of announcing*
> *the marriage of their daughter*
> *Katherine Michelle*
> *to*
> *Zachary Alan Sinclair*
> *Sunday, the twenty-seventh of November*
> *Two thousand and five*
> *Sonoma, California*

Mr. and Mrs. Joseph Anderson
and
Mr. and Mrs. Ronald Sinclair
announce
the marriage of their children
Katherine Michelle
to
Zachary Alan
Sunday, the twenty-seventh of November
Two thousand and five
Sonoma, California

Katherine Michelle Anderson

and

Zachary Alan Sinclair

have the pleasure to announce

[or announce with pleasure]

their marriage

Sunday, the twenty-seventh of November

Two thousand and five

Sonoma, California

❧ 12 ☙

Renewing Your Vows

Still madly in love after all these years? Good for you! You've got an excellent reason to celebrate, and renewing your vows is a lovely way to tell each other and the world that your spouse is still "the one." But if you think vow renewals (also called re-affirmations) are only for those married for decades, think again. While it used to be that people chose to reaffirm their vows after being married for twenty-five years or more, couples today are opting to commemorate earlier milestone anniversaries (five years, ten years, and so on) with a ceremony and party. If you're not sure what's appropriate or where to begin, read on for the latest on reaffirmation celebrations. And if you're peeking at this chapter while planning your wedding, check back in a few years!

Planning Your Celebration

There are very few "musts" or "can'ts" when it comes to a vow renewal celebration. A vow renewal can be a public event in front of loved ones or a private exchange with just you, your husband, and a presider present. You can go all out and have a "second wedding" or take a more low-key route with a small ceremony and an intimate brunch, lunch, or dinner.

Reaffirmation Styles

From big and grand to quiet and personal, the style of event you choose is up to you. Some couples opt to throw themselves a ceremony and lavish reception if they eloped or had a small wedding. Others, who had large, traditional weddings, choose to have a smaller, more casual vow renewal celebration. Some options to consider:

- A simple ceremony at your home followed by a casual lunch, dinner, or cocktails.

- A longer ceremony that includes wedding traditions such as a processional, readings, ring exchange, vows, and recessional, followed by an evening of dinner and dancing.

- A short garden ceremony followed by champagne and cake.

- A private ceremony on a cruise ship or at a vacation spot.

- A group renewal ceremony followed by a private dinner or cocktail party for friends and family. (Some houses of worship hold annual group vow renewal ceremonies and encourage couples celebrating milestone anniversaries to take part.)

Hosting the Event

Most often, the vow renewal celebration is hosted by the couple themselves or by their grown children.

When and Where

Technically, a reaffirmation can take place any time after you are married—whether you've been wed for ten years or ten days. As for the date, you can choose your anniversary date (or the closest Saturday or Sunday to it, if you prefer a weekend event) or any other date that works for you. Your ceremony can take place virtually anywhere—from the same church where you married to your own living room to a beachfront chapel during a once-in-a-lifetime vacation.

Who Does the Honors?

Anyone can preside over a vow renewal. Since it's not a legal ceremony, you don't need a clergy member or judge to preside, but many couples choose to have one. If the clergy member who performed your wedding is willing and able, asking him or her to preside over your reaffirmation is a nice touch. Other officiant options: a judge, a close friend, a relative, one of your children, or the best man or maid of honor from your wedding.

The Ceremony

One of the nice things about vow renewal ceremonies is that they can usually be customized to your personal specifications. You can design a reaffirmation ceremony that includes readings, musical selections, and an exchange of rings and vows. Or, you can simply restate your vows and exchange rings. Some couples choose to repeat the vows they made the first time because they like the idea of saying the same words they said years before.

Other couples choose to write new vows that express their current feelings and reflect on the years they've spent together.

In addition to reciting vows, exchanging rings is a key part of most reaffirmation ceremonies. You and your husband can exchange your original wedding bands again or purchase new anniversary bands to mark the occasion.

If a clergy member will preside over your reaffirmation, he or she may have some restrictions on what you can and can't include in your ceremony. Talk to him to find out if he has performed vow renewals before and what the ceremony usually includes. If you're having someone else preside, you can do virtually anything you want. For readings, you can choose scripture passages, your favorite poem, or the lyrics to a song that is special to you and your mate. The same goes for music. You can include your wedding song or any other selection that fits the occasion. Tunes like "Through the Years" and "More Today Than Yesterday" and the like are sweet songs to work into your ceremony or party.

Finally, consider hiring a professional photographer or videographer or designating a talented friend to take pictures or videotape the event. Like your wedding, this is a once-in-a-lifetime event, so don't miss the opportunity to get plenty of photos of you and your husband as well as your loved ones.

What to Wear

If your reaffirmation ceremony is designed to reflect your original wedding (say, for example, that you are using the same site and repeating the same vows), you may want to break out your original wedding gown (kudos to you if it still fits!) and ask your husband to wear the same style of tuxedo he wore for the wedding (he can update it with new accessories). If you don't want to wear your original attire, you still have plenty of options.

Not sure whether to go with a long, flowing gown or a short, simple suit? Base your attire decisions on the type of ceremony you plan to have. Here are some options:

Ceremony Style: A formal, evening celebration at a hotel, restaurant, or country club

> **You Should Wear:** A floor-length evening gown in white, ecru, ivory, platinum, or any pastel color

> **Your Husband Should Wear:** A tuxedo

Ceremony Style: A more casual affair, such as an afternoon celebration at home or at a restaurant

> **You Should Wear:** A cocktail dress, chic white pantsuit, or a beautiful dinner suit

> **Your Husband Should Wear:** A navy, dark gray, or black suit

Ceremony Style: An ultra-casual beach or backyard celebration

> **You Should Wear:** A sundress or long, flowing skirt and top

> **Your Husband Should Wear:** Khaki or gray pants and a blazer

What *Not* to Wear

Trains and veils are for first-time brides and shouldn't be worn at a reaffirmation ceremony. If you want to wear something in your hair, opt for a pretty comb, fresh flowers, or jeweled hair sticks.

Flower Power

Splurge on flowers for this special day. Whether it's a bouquet to hold as you walk down the aisle or a beautiful corsage to show that you're one of the guests of honor, pretty flowers will help set a romantic mood. Your husband can wear a fresh boutonniere on his left jacket lapel. You can even add a touch of nostalgia by asking your florist to re-create your bouquet and your husband's boutonniere from your wedding day.

Bridal Party

A bridal party isn't necessary for a vow renewal ceremony, but you may want to select attendants if you're planning an extravagant wedding-like event. If you decide to have a bridal party, you have several options: Have your children stand up for you, get your original wedding attendants to reprise their roles, or ask new friends to participate in your reaffirmation.

If you have a bridal party, you can ask the women to wear dresses of similar fabric, style, or color. It's smart to avoid bridesmaid dresses or a matching outfit for your bridesmaids, since most adult women don't feel comfortable dressing alike. As for length, the style of their dresses should match the formality of yours. If you're wearing a long gown, they can too. If you're going short, they should also. Likewise, ushers should wear attire similar in style and formality to your husband's clothing.

Including Your Children

Probably the biggest difference between your wedding and re-affirmation ceremonies is that if you have children, they most likely weren't around for the former. Since they are an integral part of your life now, though, it's nice to include them in your vow renewals in some way. Some ideas:

- Ask your children to be in your bridal party, if you're having one.

- Have your kids do readings during the ceremony. They may want to write a letter or poem for you too, which they can read aloud. Adult children can also offer toasts at the reception.

- If any of your children sings or plays an instrument, ask him or her to lend their musical talents to the day.

- If you are planning to have a processional at your ceremony, ask one or more of your children to walk down the aisle with you to meet your husband.

- Present your children with gifts to commemorate the day. A piece of jewelry or a beautifully framed family photo are two great possibilities.

The Reception

Once the ceremony is over, it's time to party! The amount of planning involved and the number of details you need to pull together will depend largely on the size and formality of your reception. If your vow renewal ceremony is a private affair for just you and your husband, the two of you can head off for a romantic meal together, or you could extend your celebration by meeting up with friends and family for a party. For a smaller, more casual at-home fete you or your host can prepare food yourself or contract a caterer to make the food. For bigger groups, you'll need to hire a caterer or hold the party at a banquet hall or other venue where food is provided.

Again, keep in mind that your reception can take any form that you would like: from big and boisterous to sentimental and serene. Whatever you decide, here are some reception ideas to keep in mind:

- Use music to set the mood. If you're having a big blowout in a ballroom or other venue, think about getting a band or DJ to perform. For a more low-key party, hire a small music group such as a jazz trio or a string quartet, or set up a CD player with your gang's favorite tunes. Even if you don't have dancing, background music provides great ambiance.

• Personalize your party by choosing a menu that reflects your life together. Did you and your husband honeymoon in Provence or live in Paris for a few years? Plan a French feast. Are you both known for your love of Mexican food? Then bring on the enchiladas and flan.

• Reenact some wedding traditions such as the first dance, receiving line (if you have a large number of guests to greet), or toasts, but nix others such as the bouquet and garter toss, which are usually just for newlyweds.

Invitations

As with any event, your invitation should match the style of your reaffirmation. For a casual affair, creating your own invitations on your computer is a great way to go. You can also find pretty fill-in-the-blank invitations at most card stores. For a more formal do, consider having invitations printed by a stationer.

Whoever is hosting the affair should issue the invitations. In most cases, that would be the celebrating couple or their children. Here's how the invitations for those scenarios would be worded:

The pleasure of your company
is requested at the reaffirmation
of the wedding vows of
Mr. and Mrs. Sean Stanhope
[or Julia and Sean Stanhope]

Saturday, the seventeenth of June
Two thousand and six
at four o'clock

Cumberland Gardens
Milford, Connecticut

The children of
Mr. and Mrs. Sean Stanhope
[or Julia and Sean Stanhope]
request the pleasure of your company
at the reaffirmation ceremony
of their parents

Saturday, the seventeenth of June
Two thousand and six
at four o'clock

At the home of Mr. and Mrs. Matthew Stanhope
Milford, Connecticut

Ann Burrows, Matthew Stanhope, and
Christine Elkins
request the pleasure of your company
at the reaffirmation ceremony
of their parents
Julia and Sean Stanhope

Saturday, the seventeenth of June
Two thousand and six
at four o'clock

The Regency Club
Rye, New York

Bring Back Good Memories

Consider invoking memories of your original nuptials, by incorporating little touches reminiscent of your wedding. Some ideas:

- Wear the jewelry you wore on your wedding day.

- Work in your original wedding colors in the linens or flowers.

- Play songs from your wedding decade—disco if you married in the 1970s and so on.

- Display some pictures from your wedding and have your wedding album on hand for guests to peruse. They will enjoy seeing how you—and they—have changed over the years.

- Have the topper from your wedding cake grace the cake at your renewal reception.

- Dance to your wedding song.

Gift Guidelines

Guests invited to celebrate your vow renewal are not required to give gifts, and if you do not want them to feel obligated to bring a present, spread the word or suggest that they make a donation to a charity instead.

Can We Talk?

Q: My husband and I are planning a vow renewal ceremony to commemorate our tenth wedding anniversary. Would it be appropriate to register for gifts like we did for our wedding?

Barbara, 40, Tennessee

A: In a word, no. Tempting as it might be, registering for gifts for a reaffirmation ceremony is inappropriate. Unlike a second or third wedding (for which couples may register), a vow renewal is simply a time to gather family and friends to celebrate the ongoing love and commitment that you and your husband share. That said, some guests may opt to bring a gift to honor this joyous occasion. In that case, you should accept their generous gift graciously and follow up with a handwritten thank-you note.

Anniversary Milestones

Traditionally, certain types of gifts were given to couples to celebrate specific anniversaries. You can use this list to work some elements of your year into your vow renewal celebration (for example, use silver as an accent color for the invitations and decorations for a twenty-fifth anniversary celebration). You may also use this list as a guide for gift-buying for your spouse or other married couples in your life.

ANNIVERSARY	TRADITIONAL	MODERN
First	Paper	Clocks
Second	Cotton	China
Third	Leather	Crystal/Glass
Fourth	Fruit/Flowers	Appliances
Fifth	Wood	Silverware
Sixth	Candy/Iron	Wood
Seventh	Wool/Copper	Desk Set
Eighth	Bronze/Pottery	Linens/Lace
Ninth	Pottery	Leather
Tenth	Tin/Aluminum	Diamond jewelry
Eleventh	Steel	Fashion jewelry
Twelfth	Silk/Linen	Pearls
Thirteenth	Lace	Textiles/Furs
Fourteenth	Ivory	Gold jewelry
Fifteenth	Crystal	Watches

ANNIVERSARY	TRADITIONAL	MODERN
Twentieth	China	Platinum
Twenty–fifth	Silver	Silver
Thirtieth	Pearl	Diamond
Thirty–fifth	Coral	Jade
Fortieth	Ruby	Ruby
Forty–fifth	Sapphire	Sapphire
Fiftieth	Gold	Gold
Fifty–fifth	Emerald	Emerald
Sixtieth	Diamond	Diamond

~ 13 ~

Wedding-Related Troubleshooting

If you start to hyperventilate at the thought of wedding-related snafus, relax! Sure, there's always a chance that something will go wrong, but in most cases it will be a minor mishap like a late limo driver or a centerpiece of flowers that is slightly different than you'd imagined. If something does go awry—the band plays the wrong song for your first dance or your hairstyle is less than perfect—remind yourself that it won't ruin this special day (heck, it may even make it more memorable!). Also keep in mind that your guests take their cue from you—if you're relaxed and having a great time, they will too.

Of course, being prepared is the best way to ensure that your day goes smoothly. Read on for practical advice for handling special wedding circumstances that may pose a few extra challenges in planning.

Planning from Afar

Couples today are on the move for school, for jobs, and for each other. So even though you live on the West Coast, you could be planning your nuptials in your New England hometown. Or maybe you moved to the Midwest to be near your fiancé, but dream of tying the knot at your Southern alma mater. Whatever the circumstances, planning a wedding in another state or even clear across the country can provide an extra challenge, but it is doable. Here are practical tips for orchestrating your wedding long distance:

- **Surf the Web.** The Internet is a great resource—and your best starting point—for long-distance planning. You can take virtual tours of reception and ceremony sites, check out the portfolios of florists, photographers, and other wedding pros, and scope out local hairstylists and makeup artists without getting in the car or on a plane. Another advantage of modern technology: You can share photos and communicate with your parents, pals, and wedding vendors via e-mail. This can be especially helpful if you're in different time zones.

- **Plan a visit to your wedding location.** After you've done your preliminary research on the Web, schedule a few days to travel to your wedding location and visit the venues and vendors you're considering. In-person meetings will help you determine whether or not you are in sync with the vendors you're thinking about hiring. Plus, some things—like menu and cake selection—just can't be done from home.

- **Ask for help.** Do your parents or siblings live near your wedding location? Is your college roommate still residing in the area? Great! Get willing friends and family members to help with local errands like picking up a marriage application or dropping your song list off with the bandleader. In-the-know locals may even be able to suggest reputable vendors and beautiful locations that you might not know about.

- **Consider hiring a wedding coordinator.** A wedding planner based where you plan to marry can be a great resource. She'll know all the best locations and most reputable and skilled wedding pros. She can also help with those details that are tough to do long-distance. Need someone to go store-to-store looking for linens that coordinate with your wedding colors? She's your woman!

- **Arrive in advance.** Get to your wedding city at least three days before the wedding. That way, you'll have plenty of time to finalize last-minute details, get a leisurely manicure and pedicure, and relax.

"Instant" Weddings

Don't have the luxury of months and months to plan your dream wedding? You're not alone. There are a number of reasons why a couple might plan a wedding in a few short months or even weeks, among them: The bride, groom, or a close family member is in the military and being deployed overseas, the couple or an immediate family member is moving a long distance, or perhaps the timing is dictated by a pregnancy, illness, or career commitments. Whatever the reason, rest assured: It really is possible to pull off a great wedding in just weeks. Keep these time-saving strategies in mind:

- **Maximize your planning time.** If possible, take a few vacation days from work so you have more time for wedding-related tasks. Also, scale back your non-wedding commitments and use the "extra" time to work on wedding to-do's like interviewing vendors and looking for a dress.

- **Become a listmaker.** Taking some time at the onset of wedding planning to get organized will save you plenty of hours and aggravation down the road. Create files for each element of your wedding—food, flowers, dresses, and so on—into which you can put brochures, swatches, and magazine pictures or articles. Also, create a master list of everything that you need to do (the time line below is a good place to start) so that you can keep track of what's accomplished and what still needs to be completed.

- **Enlist help.** Get your groom on board—he may want to take over tasks like checking out bands, interviewing photographers, and calling limousine companies. Also, delegate wedding planning jobs to willing friends and family members. For instance, ask your maid of honor to do some preliminary dress shopping for the bridal party, put Mom on flower detail, and ask your pals to help you address invitations and make favors.

- **Start with your venues.** If you're planning a religious ceremony, speak with your officiant right away to find out when he or she and/or your house of worship is available. Once you have that date, start searching out reception locations. Consider holding both your ceremony and reception in one place—that will save you the stress of trying to coordinate a date with two locations.

- **Hire your most important vendors first.** Once you have a place and a date, you can book your wedding pros. Decide which elements are most important to you—perhaps the band or the photographer—and focus on lining up those pros first.

Wedding Countdown:
Planning a Wedding in 12 weeks

Week 12

___ *Choose a first-choice date and a few alternatives.*

___ *Establish a budget.*

___ *Get ideas and referrals for your site, food, honeymoon, and so on from bridal magazines, the Internet, and friends.*

___ *Schedule appointments with potential vendors and ceremony and reception sites for the next two weeks.*

___ *Shop for a gown. (Know that buying a dress usually takes at least four months, but some stores can handle rush orders for an additional fee. Also consider buying your dress off the rack or purchasing a dress shop sample that is in excellent condition.)*

Week 11

___ *Book your ceremony and reception venues.*

___ *Book as many professionals as you can, like the officiant, florist, caterer, and band.*

___ *Ask people to be in your bridal party.*

___ *Order invitations.*

___ *Choose and order rings.*

___ *Reserve hotel rooms for out-of-town guests.*

___ *Book your honeymoon.*

Week 10

___ Hire any remaining vendors.

___ Buy dress and accessories.

___ Book a hair and makeup stylist for the day of the wedding
and appointments for a manicure and pedicure for the day
before the wedding.

___ Get blood tests (if required—talk to your officiant).

Week 9

___ Send invitations.

___ Select bridesmaid dresses.

___ Have your fiancé shop for tuxes for himself and his
groomsmen.

Week 8

___ Register for gifts.

Week 7

___ Meet with the officiant to plan the ceremony.

___ Book and/or confirm ceremony musicians.

Week 6

___ Meet with your caterer to taste foods and plan the menu.

___ Book limousines or car service.

Week 5

___ Give bandleader or DJ a list of music you want played.

___ Get your marriage license.

Week 4

___ Have a dress fitting (you'll have to follow the store's schedule).

___ Make sure you have all your accessories.

Week 3

___ Find something old, new, borrowed, and blue.

___ Pick up rings.

Week 2

___ Contact guests who have not RSVP'd.

___ Make reception seating arrangements.

Week 1

___ Pick up your dress.

___ Confirm wedding services.

___ Give final head count to your caterer.

___ Start packing for the honeymoon.

Wedding Countdown: Planning Your Wedding in Six Weeks or Less

Week 6

___ Announce your engagement.

___ Set your budget.

___ Decide on a guest list.

___ Research sites for ceremony and reception.

___ Call vendors and set up appointments.

___ Choose your bridal party.

___ Shop for a dress.

Week 5

___ Book ceremony and reception site(s).

___ Hire as many of your wedding professionals as you can (caterer, florist, photographer, musicians, etc.).

___ Order invitations.

___ Order rings.

___ Reserve hotel rooms for out-of-town guests.

___ Book your honeymoon.

___ Register for gifts.

Week 4

___ Mail invitations.

___ Buy dress and accessories.

___ Shop for bridesmaid dresses.

___ *Have fiancé select tuxes for himself and men in bridal party.*

___ *Meet with your officiant to plan ceremony.*

___ *Book limousines/car service.*

___ *Finish hiring the rest of your wedding professionals.*

Week 3

___ *Book hairstylist and makeup artist.*

Week 2

___ *Meet with caterer to plan menu.*

___ *Give DJ or bandleader a list of music you want played.*

___ *Get your marriage license.*

Week 1

___ *Give caterer final head count.*

___ *Determine reception seating.*

___ *Have final dress fitting.*

___ *Pick up dress.*

___ *Pick up rings.*

___ *Finalize any last-minute details.*

___ *Pack for your honeymoon.*

Rain, Rain, Go Away!

You can't control Mother Nature—though many a bride has wished she could! Whether your wedding day is wet (or snowy or sweltering) is out of your hands, but you should be prepared for the possibility of bad weather. If you're planning an outdoor ceremony or reception, always have a Plan B that includes an alternate place to hold the wedding. Rain is the most common scenario, but an extreme heat wave could be just as troublesome. Consider having a large, waterproof canopy on hold at a local rental company in case of rain. For too-hot weather, large rented fans can be a lifesaver. If you need to move the ceremony indoors, station an usher near where guests will arrive so he can direct them to the new location.

Did You Know?

According to Hindu tradition, rain on your wedding day is actually said to be good luck!

Bright Idea

If it rains on your wedding day, hand out inexpensive parasols (go for white or a color that coordinates with your wedding) to guests who arrive without umbrellas. Celebrity wedding planner Mindy Weiss ties a note to the umbrella handle that says, "Rain, rain, go away. But you won't spoil our wedding day."

Tipping Guide

Knowing who to tip and how much can be confusing, and it can be embarrassing to be caught short. Some gratuities are included in the fees you are charged up front. Others are given at your discretion when services are performed. So before handing out any cash, check your contracts to see if tips are included. The best way to give a tip to a vendor? Enclose cash or a check in an envelope with a thank-you note (do this ahead of time). The best man can give the officiant and others who participated in the ceremony their envelopes following the ceremony. You or your groom can distribute the envelope to pros working at your reception, after the party winds down. While it's nice for the bride and groom to give out the tips personally, it's okay to ask a trusted friend or family member to do it if you can't.

PARTICIPANT	HOW MUCH	WHO PAYS
Clergy member (priest, minister, rabbi)	Usually a donation ($25 to $100), depending on ceremony size.	The groom gives the donation to the best man, who pays after the ceremony.
Public official (judge, justice of the peace, city clerk)	Usually a flat fee ($25 and up): Some judges cannot accept money.	The groom gives the money to the best man, who pays after the ceremony.
Ceremony assistants (altar boys, sextons, cantors, organists)	Often covered by the church/synagague fee, but check with your clergy member to find out what is customary (usually $5 to $25).	If included in the church fee, the ceremony host pays when billed. If not, give the tip after the service.

PARTICIPANT	HOW MUCH	WHO PAYS
Limousine driver	15–20 percent, unless it is included in the contract price.	Reception host can add tip on the day of service.
Florist, baker, photographer, musicians	Only tipped for special service (i.e., if they go above and beyond what is expected).	Reception host can add tip on the day of service.
Hairstylist and makeup artist	15–20 percent of their fees.	The person paying for the service should tip at the time of the service.
Waiters, waitresses, bartenders, table captains, maitre d'	15 percent for servers; 1–2 percent for captains; 15–20 percent for maître d'.	If included, the reception host pays tips with the bill. If not, pay after the reception.
Restroom attendants	50 cents to $1 per guest, or arrange a flat fee with hosts. Pay it with the bill.	If a flat fee, the reception host pays it with the bill. If not, pay before the reception so that guests are not expected to tip.
Coatroom attendants	50 cents to $1 per coat, or arrange a flat fee with the hotel or club.	If a flat fee, the reception host pays it with the bill. If not, pay before the reception so that guests are not expected to tip.

PARTICIPANT	HOW MUCH	WHO PAYS
Car valets	$1–$3 per car, unless it is included in the contract price.	If included, the reception host pays tips with the bill. If not, pay after the reception. Keep in mind that the number of cars isn't the same as the number of guests. For example, there may be about 75 cars for a wedding with 200 guests.

If the host pays the tips for the bartenders, coatroom attendants, restroom attendants, and car valets before the reception or as part of the total bill, be sure there are no baskets on the bar, at coat check, near the valet stand, or in restrooms that would make guests feel they should tip.

"What Should I Do If...?"

From time to time, situations arise that can test even an etiquette expert's grace under fire. The golden rule of etiquette—be courteous to and considerate of others—always applies, but let's face it, some circumstances call for more specific advice. When something happens that makes you think, "Aagh! What should I do?" take a deep breath and follow the advice below for handling some common quandaries.

Including In-Laws

Sticky Situation: Your future in-laws feel left out of the wedding planning.

Savvy Solution: Reach out to your fiancé's folks by e-mailing pictures of the reception site or calling them with telephone updates about the wedding plans. Since the couple or the bride's family often take the lead in wedding planning, it can be hard for the groom's family (especially if they don't live near the couple or the wedding location) to feel included. Reaching out to your future in-laws is a nice gesture—and a smart move since you'll be part of each other's lives for years to come.

Date Demands

Sticky Situation: A guest asks to bring an (uninvited) date.

Savvy Solution: The rule of thumb on guests and dates: Invite singles with dates who are engaged, living with someone, or have long-term significant others. If a guest doesn't fall into any of these categories but asks to bring a date, it is perfectly fine to decline the request. Simply explain that your plans only allow for a certain number of guests, and as much as you would like to have included the date, it's just not possible. End of story.

Mom's Way or the Highway

Sticky Situation: Your mom has definite ideas about every detail of your wedding, and what she wants is wildly different from what you want.

Savvy Solution: Your mom may have been imagining your wedding since the day the doctor told her, "It's a girl!" And if she and/or your dad are paying for this shindig she may feel she has a right to call the shots. Your first move: Sit your mom down for a heartfelt chat. Explain that you really appreciate her enthusiasm but that you want to have a celebration that reflects you and your fiancé. Compromise is the name of the game, so reassure your mom that you won't cut her out of the process entirely. Instead, divvy up the duties into areas that you can each be "in charge" of. For example, if having a chic sheath dress instead of the traditional ball gown your mom prefers is important to you, hold your ground. But if you don't have strong feelings on, say, the linens or the flowers, let Mom get her way. Bottom line: You want to come out of this experience with a wedding you loved and a solid relationship with your mother.

Uninvited and Unhappy

Sticky Situation: A coworker or acquaintance is upset about not being invited to the wedding.

Savvy Solution: It can be difficult to exclude people from your guest list, but the fact is it's usually impossible to invite everyone you know. Your best bet: Avoid talking about the wedding with those who aren't invited. Of course, you're excited about your upcoming event, but it's unfair to go on about a cake and flowers you know this person will never see. If someone approaches you to say she is upset about being excluded, gently explain that unfortunately you weren't able to invite everyone you would have liked, but that you hope to have her friendship and good wishes. Also, keep in mind that with coworkers it's often best to take an all-or-nothing approach to inviting them. Excluding just one or two people from a group you lunch with regularly is bound to cause resentment. Also, be sure to invite your supervisor and assistant. And, if you are head of a large department and can't possibly invite everyone who works for you, then ask only the most senior members of the group.

Pushy Parents

Sticky Situation: A friend or relative wants to bring her three-year-old to an adults-only wedding.

Savvy Solution: Once you've made the decision not to invite children to your wedding (which is perfectly acceptable), you can't make any exceptions or you'll be setting yourself up for problems with other guests who have children. Explain to the parent that the reception is only for adults, but that she's welcome to bring her child to the ceremony. You can also recommend a trustworthy babysitter near your wedding location.

Are You Coming or Not?

Sticky Situation: The RSVP date for your wedding has come and gone with no response from several guests.

Savvy Solution: In an ideal world, all guests would let you know if they are accepting or declining your invitation by the RSVP date. In reality, you'll have to call the stragglers to find out if they are planning to attend so you can map out the seating arrangements and provide your caterer with a final head count. Enlist the help of your parents, your groom, and your future in-laws. Each person can call any of "their" guests who haven't responded.

Guest List Overload

Sticky Situation: Your in-laws are insisting on inviting more than their allotted number of guests.

Savvy Solution: Have your fiancé speak to his parents, and explain that while you'd love to include everyone on their list, your budget only allows for them to invite "x number" of people. If they won't cut their list, he can offer them two alternatives: They can pay for the dinners for their additional guests, or they can create an A-list and a B-list. Invitations can go out to people on their B-list as regrets come in from the A-list invitees. That way, your in-laws will be able to include as many of their family and friends as possible—without causing a budget meltdown.

Divorce Dilemma

Sticky Situation: Your divorced parents can barely stand being in the same room together, never mind planning a wedding.

Savvy Solution: Talk to your parents (or have your fiancé speak with his parents, if they are the issue) about your concerns. They may not realize how much pain their tension is causing you. Remind them that this is an important time in your life—one that you want to look back on fondly—and ask if they can put aside their bitter feelings. Also, find out from each of them how they would like to participate in the wedding (Are they comfortable co-hosting? Would one prefer to host?) so that you can work out a compromise with which everyone will be comfortable. When it comes to seating, plan for one parent (usually the mother) to be seated in the first row and the other parent to be seated in the third row during the ceremony. At the reception, each parent can host a separate table. So while your parents should be civil to one another, reassure them that you don't expect them to act like a happily married couple.

Feeling Faint

Sticky Situation: You or a member of the wedding party feels faint during the ceremony.

Savvy Solution: Quickly step away and find somewhere to sit down. (Before the wedding, place a chair on either side of the altar or huppah in case someone needs to sit.) Once seated, take several deep breaths. Don't try to tough it out if you're feeling light-headed; it's better to graciously step away than to faint during the ceremony. A final word of advice: An empty stomach can lead to dizziness, so minimize your fainting risk by fueling up with a healthy breakfast (try scrambled eggs and toast or fruit and oatmeal) on the morning of the wedding.

Having Too Good of a Time

Sticky Situation: An intoxicated guest is making a spectacle of himself at the reception.

Savvy Solution: Handling drunken guests can be tricky, so your best bet is often to let the maître d', who is likely experienced in this type of situation, run interference. Since a drunk guest can't leave on his or her own and may refuse a cab ride or a ride from a friend, the safest plan is often to remove the guest from the party, but not the reception location itself. For example, you can have a staff member or a friend (or your wedding coordinator, if you have one) escort the guest from the ballroom to a lounge area or separate room and isolate the person there (a friend or two can sit with the person if that helps) until he or she sobers up and calms down.

From Toast to Roast

Sticky Situation: A toast starts out well but quickly turns sour because of foul language or inappropriate anecdotes.

Savvy Solution: One of the best man's jobs is to manage the toasts, so if a guest's ramblings need to be cut off, he's the one who should intervene to end the toast. If the best man is the offensive speaker, the groom or an usher can step in and retrieve the microphone.

Your Wedding Emergency Kit

You, darling, must be prepared for anything that comes your way on your big day. Arm yourself with the tools listed below and nothing—be it a ripped hem or squeaky shoes—will keep you from wedding day enjoyment.

Double-stick fabric tape
Perfect for fixing fallen hems or fastening bra straps that keep peeking out of your gown or your bridesmaids' dresses.

Moleskin
Use a piece as padding for sore feet.

Scissors
To cut moleskin and fabric tape.

Superglue
Among its uses: repairing shoe heels that snap off and fingernails that break.

Baby powder
Great for stopping shoes from squeaking as you walk.

Hairspray
For fast hair repair.

Ibuprofen
A quick fix for headaches.

Deodorant
Handy to have for touch-ups throughout the day.

Breath mints
They help with dry mouth, and keep your breath sweet for greeting guests and your first kiss as husband and wife.

Toothbrush and toothpaste
Step away to brush between the cocktail hour and reception and/or after dinner to freshen up.

Straws
Sip drinks through a straw to avoid ruining your lipstick.

Small sewing kit
Include thread in white and the color of your bridesmaids' dresses to quickly repair last-minute tears.

Clear nail polish
Use it to stop pantyhose runs in their tracks.

Tissues
For tears and tons of other uses.

No Smoking Section

Sticky Situation: Several guests light up cigarettes after dinner—to the dismay of other guests seated nearby.

Savvy Solution: You can avoid this scenario by prearranging a place for smokers to light up away from other guests. Good options: lobby, lounge, or outdoor terrace. Simply instruct the waitstaff to politely direct guests to these designated areas when they want to smoke.

Postponing the Wedding

From time to time, couples find their wedding must be postponed due to illness, cold feet, a family situation, or another reason. If you're in that situation, it is important to notify your guests promptly. The decision about how to let them know of the postponement will most likely be based on how far away the scheduled wedding date is.

If the invitations have been printed but not yet mailed, you can include in the invitation envelope a printed card stating the new date. For example, "The date of the wedding has been changed from June 19, 2005, to September 10, 2005."

If the invitations have already been mailed and the original wedding date is still several weeks away, you can send a printed card to announce the postponement.

If you don't know the new date, use this wording:

Mr. and Mrs. Charles Luna
announce that the marriage of
their daughter
Samantha Renee
to
Christopher Martinez
has been postponed

If you do know the new date, write:

Mr. and Mrs. Charles Luna
announce that the marriage of
their daughter
Samantha Renee
to
Christopher Martinez
has been postponed to
the tenth of September
Two thousand and five

If the wedding is just a few days away, call or e-mail guests to alert them to the change in plans.

Canceling the Wedding

If you find that you need to cancel the wedding completely, you'll also need to notify your guests. If the wedding is canceled after the invitations have been sent out, you have two options: Send out a printed card informing guests of the cancellation or, if there's no time for that (if the wedding is, say, a week away), notify guests via phone or e-mail. The last thing you'd probably feel like doing is telling people your wedding is off, so ask a close friend or family member to take charge of getting the word out to guests.

How to word cancellation notices:

Mr. and Mrs. Charles Luna
announce that the marriage of
their daughter
Samantha Renee
to
Christopher Martinez
will not take place

OR

The wedding of
Samantha Luna
and
Christopher Martinez
will not take place

Other Cancellation Issues

Besides notifying the guests of the cancellation, all engagement, shower, and wedding gifts should be returned to the givers
within a few weeks of the broken engagement. Include a brief
note thanking the giver and stating that you are returning the
gift because the wedding has been canceled—you don't need to
go into detail or offer a reason for the cancellation.

Did You Know?

In most states, a woman must return her engagement
ring, regardless of why or by whom the engagement
was called off. This is based on the premise that an
engagement ring is a gift on condition of marriage
and if that condition is not met for any reason, the
ring should be returned. If a woman doesn't return
the ring, her ex-groom can take legal action, though
this is rare. One exception: By law in Montana, a
woman can keep the ring.

Another issue to be dealt with is canceling wedding-related
orders and services (again, a trusted friend or relative can handle
these tasks). Read each of your vendor contracts carefully to
understand the cancellation policy. Depending on when you

cancel, you will probably have to forfeit some or all of your deposits. Contact your dress shop to see if it is possible to cancel your order (if your gown hasn't already come in). If it's too late to cancel, your dress shop may be able to sell your gown at a sample sale. Bringing your dress to a consignment shop is another option. Finally, you aren't responsible for reimbursing your bridesmaids for their dresses (and if they are your closest friends, they'll be more worried about you than the money), but find out if you can cancel the order for dresses that haven't yet arrived.

Simple Stress Busters for Anxious Brides

This probably won't come as news to you, but getting married can be extremely stressful. Not only are you making a till-death-do-you-part commitment, but the multitude of planning details is enough to drive even the most organized bride-to-be batty. When you feel your stress level rising, try these tension tamers:

- **Exercise away tension.** If a stress-induced meltdown is coming on, go out for a walk or run, pop in your favorite fitness video, or challenge your fiancé to a game of tennis.

- **Nosh on good-mood food.** Comfort foods like macaroni and cheese, mashed potatoes, and chocolate chip cookies can help soothe frayed nerves by reminding you of happy childhood memories. These treats are fine on occasion, but also consider healthier options such as low-fat ice cream with granola, sherbet topped with fruit, or baked tortilla chips and salsa, which won't compromise your wedding-dress diet.

- **Record and release.** Trying to remember a million different details and to-do's is mentally taxing. Instead, stash paper all around—your purse, the bathroom, your car—so you can jot down ("record") things you need to do and then forget them until later ("release"), instead of struggling to remember everything.

- **Get to bed on time.** When things get hectic, sleep often gets sacrificed. Help yourself stay sane by getting enough sleep every night.

- **Schedule a night out with your fiancé or friends.** Taking a break from your wedding worries to hang out with friends or your fiancé is a great way to decompress. Head out to your favorite restaurant, rent a funny movie, or hit the mall for some retail therapy.

- **Spend time with your family.** Research has shown that participating in family rituals such as eating together can be comforting during stressful times, so drop by Mom and Dad's for a Sunday dinner or a weekend game night.

- **Enlist help.** Don't feel that you need to handle the flowers, the music, the menu, and the guest list solo. Ask your parents, your fiancé, and your friends for help. No doubt they'll be happy to pitch in, and delegating will take some of the pressure off you.

- **Imagine your honeymoon.** When stress threatens to overshadow the joy of your wedding, take a few minutes to visualize yourself and your man enjoying your honeymoon trip. Picture the two of you relaxing on the sand in Fiji or enjoying a gourmet Italian meal in Florence. Aah, that's better!

The First Year of Marriage

The champagne has been sipped, the wedding cake devoured, and the honeymoon enjoyed. Whew! Now there's just one thing left to do: Make like a fairy-tale bride, and live happily ever after. Sound like a tall order? It can be. Adjusting to married life takes time, communication, and compromise. Chances are, during your engagement many people—from your mom, to sisters, to married friends—spent hours talking with you about fondant, flowers, and fonts for your invitation. But there's one thing they may have forgotten to mention: Marriage is a huge adjustment. And with your thoughts consumed by wedding details, it's easy to forget that there is life after the last dance. But don't worry, you're not alone. Though navigating the waters of newlywed life can be full of ups and downs, you don't have to do it alone. You and your best friend—your new hubby—have each other.

Besides, you can think of your wedding planning as good preparation for married life. The same diplomacy that helped you tactfully explain to your mother-in-law that you wouldn't be inviting all thirty-seven of her cousins to the wedding can guide you through the tricky issues you'll face as a newlywed. Read on for more straight talk about the joys and challenges of the first year of marriage.

Post-Honeymoon Hangover

You had a gorgeous wedding and a fabulous honeymoon and now you and the man you love are back to "normal." Then why do you feel so, well, abnormal? Relax, it's not uncommon for newlyweds to feel down once all the gifts are put away and the guests have gone home. After being "the bride" and getting feted with parties and showered with gifts, returning to real life can be a letdown. For most people, going to work every day certainly isn't as much fun as tasting wedding cakes or parasailing in the islands!

Besides the post-party letdown, embarking on your new married life means you have to say good-bye to singlehood, and that can feel like a loss in some ways. Even though you are excited to become part of a married couple, you are trading in your familiar identity as an independent, single person. Working late every night or meeting your girlfriends for happy hour may not be as appealing when you have your new hubby to go home to—but that doesn't mean you won't miss the daily gabfests with your friends or the camaraderie with your coworkers. Even when you're happy about the changes in your life, it can still be hard to leave behind parts of your "old life."

If your new status as a wife (even the word takes a little while to get used to!) starts to feel a little overwhelming, remember that marriage, like any other transitional stage in life, such as going to college or starting a new job, requires an adjustment period. Give yourself a week or so to experience your post-honeymoon hangover. Relax, get plenty of rest, and you should start to feel like your old self again soon. If possible, avoid making other big changes right now. This may not be the right time to buy a house or change jobs, unless you really have to, since you are still getting used to the big shifts that come with marriage. Another break-out-of-that-funk fix: Give yourself something new to look forward to by planning activities with your husband, family, and friends. Invite your pals over for your first dinner party as a married couple, book a weekend at a romantic bed-and-breakfast for your six-month anniversary, or start a home renovation project you wanted to do but didn't have time for during the wedding planning rush. Instead of focusing on the end of your wedding, think about the beginning of your life together!

Transitioning from "Me" to "We"

One of the biggest challenges of going from a single person to half of a married couple is adjusting your thinking from "me" to "we." As a single person, you had more leeway to do what you wanted when you wanted. That's not to say that getting married means giving up your independence and quashing your desires in favor of your husband's, just that you need to be aware that you're no longer the only factor in the equation. Here, some common newlywed hot-button issues and advice for dealing.

Holiday Hijinks

Maybe you've gone to your grandparents' house in Vermont every Christmas for the last twenty years, while your husband always spends Christmas morning unwrapping gifts around his parents' Christmas tree in Houston. Working out a holiday solution everyone can live with can be tricky. Besides your desires and your husband's, you also have to contend with input from your families as well. Your best bet: Sit down with your hubby and calmly craft a plan. Many couples find that alternating holidays works well. For example, one year you spend Thanksgiving with your family, Hanukkah with his, and Passover with yours. The next year, you do the opposite. For other couples—those with both families within driving distance, for example—splitting each holiday works best. That means Thanksgiving dinner may be at your parents' home and then you head to your in-laws for dessert. Another option: Host a holiday in your own home and invite both families to participate.

Whatever plan you adopt, present a united front when sharing your decision with your families. In most cases, it's best for you to inform your folks ("Tom and I are going to spend this Easter with his family, but we'll be spending next Easter with you.") and have your husband talk to his. One final piece of advice: Don't wait until the last minute to apprise relatives of your plan. People are apt to be less disappointed if they know in advance what to expect.

Keeping Confidences

Think twice if you're used to confiding in your mom, sis, or pal about every aspect of your life. Once you're married (and even at times when you're engaged), there are certain things that should stay between your husband and you. Mad that he blew a bundle on a plasma TV? Venting to your best friend may not be the best idea. Instead, focus on working through the issue with your husband. Just as you wouldn't want him sharing details about your life with his buddies (Do they really need to know that you got demoted at work?), he needs to know that you will respect his confidences.

Financial Feuds

Money can be a hugely divisive issue for many couples—in fact, it's the number one reason couples in America divorce. Why? They don't adequately communicate about their expectations, spending styles, and so on, so they never get in sync about money. Take advantage of this formative stage of your marriage to get off on the right foot, financially speaking. Even before the wedding, sit down together and discuss the big issues: Will you have separate accounts or a joint one? Who will be responsible for paying the bills? Do you need to check with each other before making big purchases? How will you decide how much of your income to spend and how much to save? Beware that you bring your own family's money-handling history into your marriage and your husband brings his. Maybe your dad deposited every paycheck into a joint account and your mom handled the bills with no questions asked by your dad. You may expect things to run the same way in your household, while your new husband plans to monitor the finances closely the way his dad did. Talk about these patterns and decide how things will work in your marriage. For help, consider talking to a financial planner for advice on setting up a workable system.

Intimacy Issues

Sex is another hot topic for many couples. You and your husband may have very different views on what constitutes a satisfying sex life. Take the time to discuss your expectations. Also, it's easy to get caught up in the minutiae of daily life and let sex and romance slide, but don't give into that temptation. Check out the following tips for keeping your relationship hot post-honeymoon.

Friendly Competition

You have a monthly spa day with your best friend. He's got a regular poker night. Each of you probably has traditions with your friends that you want to maintain even after you're married. And that's great. Getting married doesn't mean giving up your pals—and your marriage can even benefit from some time apart. Just be sure each of you is comfortable with the balance between friend time and couple time. And remember that there's no formula for a good husband or wife. For some couples, vacationing without each other is unthinkable, but for others getting away for the weekend with the girls while he goes golfing with his brother and dad is perfectly fine. Trial and error will help you determine what's right for the two of you. Also, make an effort to meet some shared couple friends to supplement "his" friends and "your" friends.

Reasonable Boundaries

Maybe you never minded when your mom called your apartment at eight in the morning on a Saturday, but if the ringing phone gets your hubby's weekend off to a bad start, it's time to reevaluate. Decide between the two of you what things are acceptable (Is dropping by unannounced okay or do you want your families to call first? Are you going to continue having dinner with your parents every Sunday or not?) and, again, present a united front when informing your families of your choices. Don't put one another in the position of "bad guy." Saying, "Sorry, Mom, but Ryan doesn't want you to call on Saturday mornings" sets up a him versus them mentality between your husband and your family—a sure recipe for disaster. A better choice of wording: "Ryan and I like to relax on Saturday mornings, so it would be great if you could wait until at least noon to call us."

How to Fight Fair

Let's be honest: Virtually all couples argue, be it over small annoyances like forgotten chores or larger issues like where to buy a house or how to spend that tax refund check. Since disagreements are inevitable, you might as well figure out how to work through them wisely. Keep these tips in mind the next time an argument erupts:

- **Get a grip.** When you feel as if your head is going to explode in anger, it's not the best time to air your grievances. You run too high a risk of saying something you may regret later. Instead, get some space from your mate and gather your thoughts. You can jot down why you're upset and even practice what you'll say so that you're calmer and more focused when you discuss the situation with your husband.

- **Steer clear of accusations and generalizations.** Saying, "You always favor your family over mine. You're not a good son-in-law" will automatically put your man on the defensive. A better option: Express how you feel, not what you see as your partner's shortcomings. "I feel hurt when I want to have dinner with my family and you don't want to" is the opener to a more productive conversation.

- **Acknowledge your partner's anger.** You don't have to agree with his points, but you should let him know you're listening and that you understand that he's upset. Phrases like "I hear what you're saying" and "I see you are upset about that" can help diffuse his anger.

Keep the Romance Alive

It's easy to feel romantic when you're eating a private dinner for two on the beach in Bali at sunset. Harder is maintaining that loving feeling after coming home from a long day of school or work and popping a meal for two in the microwave. Here, some tips on keeping the fire stoked long after you've returned from your honeymoon:

- **Make use of the those wedding gifts.** Break out those crystal candlesticks you received and light a set of tapers to create a romantic glow, or surprise each other with a great meal (if you're not a cook, takeout works!) on your good dishes.

- **Create your own rituals.** Start a habit of spending leisurely Sunday mornings sharing coffee, bagels, and the newspaper. Make Friday or Saturday date night and aim to try a new restaurant each week or hit the tennis courts on Saturday mornings.

- **Practice random acts of kindness.** Sure, sweeping your sweetie off for a romantic weekend in Paris is a great way to let him know you love him, but don't underestimate the value of small, loving gestures like giving him a massage when he's stressed about work or taking over trash duties so he can sleep later one morning. It's these everyday kindnesses that remind each of you that some-one is looking out for you.

- **Break out of a rut.** Dinner-and-a-movie dates are fine, but they can get a little, well, boring. Instead of the same old standbys, why not branch out and try a cook-ing class for two, learn a foreign language together (Learning French can be très romantique!), or packing a picnic to take hiking? Mixing it up will keep your relationship fresh.

Don't leave your sex life on your honeymoon. Finding the time and energy for sex can be a challenge when you've got bills to pay, groceries to buy, and jobs to head off to every day. Make a pact to carve out time for intimacy, even going so far as scheduling it in your date books.

Loving Your Newlywed Life

Married life can be a lot of work, but it's also a tremendous amount of fun. After all, you now have a built-in partner for all your crazy adventures and quiet times. Whether you're exploring a new place on vacation or just vegging out on the couch at home, you'll be doing it with your best friend. Anticipate some adjustment anxiety, but try to relax and enjoy this special time in your lives!

Appendix A: *How to Word Your Engagement Announcement*

When the Bride's Parents Are Divorced and One Parent Is Making the Announcement

Mrs. Annette Johnson announces the engagement of her daughter, Suzanne Marie Johnson, to Scott Thompson, son of Mr. and Mrs. Robert Thompson of Albuquerque, New Mexico. Miss Johnson is also the daughter of Mr. Kenneth Johnson of Orlando, Florida.

Note: In this case, the parent who raised you should announce the engagement, and the other parent should be mentioned later.

When the Bride's Parents Are Divorced and Both Are Making the Announcement

Mrs. Annette Johnson of Cambridge, Massachusetts, and Mr. Kenneth Johnson of Orlando, Florida, announce the engagement of their daughter, Suzanne Marie Johnson, to Scott Thompson, son of Mr. and Mrs. Robert Thompson of Albuquerque, New Mexico.

When the Groom's Parents Are Divorced

Mr. and Mrs. Kenneth Johnson of Cambridge, Massachusetts, announce the engagement of their daughter, Suzanne Marie Johnson, to Scott Thompson, son of Mrs. Carolyn Hunt of Fairfield, Connecticut, and Mr. Robert Thompson of Albuquerque, New Mexico.

When One of the Bride's Parents Is Deceased

The engagement of Suzanne Marie Johnson, daughter of Mrs. Kenneth Johnson of Cambridge, Massachusetts, and the late Mr. Johnson, to Scott Thompson, son of Mr. and Mrs. Robert Thompson of Albuquerque, New Mexico, is announced by the bride's mother.

OR

Mrs. Kenneth Johnson of Cambridge, Massachusetts, announces the engagement of her daughter, Suzanne Marie Johnson, to Scott Thompson, son of Mr. and Mrs. Robert Thompson of Albuquerque, New Mexico. Ms. Johnson is also the daughter of the late Kenneth Johnson.

When One of the Groom's Parents Is Deceased

Mr. and Mrs. Kenneth Johnson of Cambridge, Massachusetts, announce the engagement of their daughter, Suzanne Marie Johnson, to Scott Thompson, son of Mrs. Robert Thompson and the late Robert Thompson.

When One Parent Is Deceased and a Stepparent Is Mentioned

The engagement of Suzanne Marie Johnson, daughter of Mrs. Annette Johnson Walters and the late Kenneth Johnson, and stepdaughter of Mr. James Walters, to Scott Thompson, son of Mr. and Mrs. Robert Thompson of Albuquerque, New Mexico, is announced by the bride's parents.

For a Second Marriage

Mr. and Mrs. Kenneth Johnson announce the engagement of their daughter, Suzanne Johnson Harvey [or Suzanne Harvey], to Scott Thompson, son of Mr. and Mrs. Robert Thompson of Albuquerque, New Mexico.

Note: In this case, "Harvey" is the bride's name from her first marriage. This would be used if she changed her name when she married the first time, and didn't revert to her maiden name when she divorced.

Engagement Announcement Forms

Basic Engagement Announcement

_____ of _____ announce
    Names of Bride's Parents   *City/State Where Parents Reside*

the engagement of their daughter, _____, to
    Bride's Name

_____, son of _____
    Groom's Name   *Names of Groom's Parents*

of _____.
    City/State Where Groom's Parents Reside

The bride graduated _____
    Include honors such as summa cum laude, etc., if applicable

from _____, where she received her _____
    Name of College/University   *Cite Degree*

in _____. She is a _____ at
    Subject of Degree/Major   *Job Title*

_____ in _____.
    Business Name   *City/State Where Business is Located*

The groom graduated _____
    Include honors such as summa cum laude, etc., if applicable

from _____, where he received his _____
    Name of College/University   *Cite Degree*

in _____. He is a _____ at
    Subject of Degree/Major   *Job Title*

_____ in _____.
    Business Name   *City/State Where Business is Located*

A _____ wedding is planned [or "a wedding date has not yet
    Month of Wedding

been set."]

For more information, please contact:

_____
    Bride or Groom's Name

_____
    Address

_____
    Work Phone

_____
    Home Phone

_____
    E-mail

Basic Engagement Announcement When Bride and/or Groom Has a Graduate Degree

_____ of _____ announce the
Names of Bride's Parents   City/State Where Parents Reside

engagement of their daughter, _____, to
Bride's Name

_____, son of _____
Groom's Name   Names of Groom's Parents

of _____.
City/State Where Groom's Parents Reside

The bride graduated _____
Include honors such as summa cum laude, etc., if applicable

from _____, where she received her _____
Name of College/University   Cite Degree

in _____ and _____ from
Subject of Degree/Major   Include honors such as summa cum laude, etc., if applicable

_____, where she received her _____ in
Name of College/University   Cite Degree

_____. She is a _____ at
Subject of Degree/Major   Job Title

_____ in _____.
Business Name   City/State Where Business is Located

The groom graduated _____
Include honors such as summa cum laude, etc., if applicable

from _____, where he received his _____ in
Name of College/University   Cite Degree

_____, and _____ from
Subject of Degree/Major   Include honors such as summa cum laude, etc., if applicable

_____, where he received his _____ in
Name of College/University   Cite Degree

_____. He is a _____ at
Subject of Degree/Major   Job Title

_____ in _____.
Business Name   City/State Where Business is Located

A _____ wedding is planned [or "a wedding date has not yet
Month of Wedding

been set."]

For more information, please contact:

_____
Bride or Groom's Name

_____
Address

_____
Work Phone

_____
Home Phone

_____
E-mail

Basic Engagement Announcement by the Couple

_____, a _____at
Bride's Name Job Title

_____in _____,
Business Name City/State Where Business is Located

is to be married to _____, a _____
Groom's Name Job Title

at _____ in _____.
Business Name City/State Where Business is Located

The bride is the daughter of _____of
Names of Bride's Parents

_____.
City/State Where Parents Reside

The groom is the son of _____ of
Names of Groom's Parents

_____.
City/State Where Groom's Parents Reside

A _____ wedding is planned [or "a wedding date
Month of Wedding

has not yet been set."]

For more information, please contact:

_____
Bride or Groom's Name

_____
Address

_____
Work Phone

_____
Home Phone

_____
E-mail

Detailed Engagement Announcement by the Couple

_____, a _____at
Bride's Name   Job Title

_____ in _____, is engaged to
Business Name   City/State Where Business is Located

marry, _____, a _____ at
Groom's Name   Job Title

_____in _____. The bride
Business Name   City/State Where Business is Located

graduated _____ from _____,
Include honors such as summa cum laude, etc., if applicable   Name of College/University

where she received her _____ in _____.
Cite Degree   Subject of Degree/Major

The groom graduated _____ from
Include honors such as summa cum laude, etc., if applicable

_____, where he received his _____
Name of College/University   Cite Degree

in _____.
Subject of Degree/Major

Ms. _____ is the daughter of _____
Bride's Name   Names of Bride's Parents

of _____. Her father is a _____.
City/State Where Parents Reside   Name of Profession or Retired Profession

Her mother is a _____.
Name of Profession or Retired Profession

Mr. _____ is the son of _____ of
Groom's Name   Names of Groom's Parents

_____. His father is a _____.
City/State Where Groom's Parents Reside   Name of Profession or Retired Profession

His mother is a _____.
Name of Profession or Retired Profession

A _____wedding is planned in _____.
Month of Wedding   City/State Where Wedding Will Be Held

The couple plans to reside in _____ .
City/State Where You Plan to Live

For more information, please contact:

_____
Bride or Groom's Name

_____
Address

_____
Work Phone

_____
Home Phone

_____
E-mail

Detailed Engagement Announcement by Couple
with Graduate Degrees

_____, a _____ at
Bride's Name Job Title

_____ in _____, is engaged to
Business Name City/State Where Business is Located

marry _____, a _____
Groom's Name Job Title

at _____ in _____.
Business Name City/State Where Business is Located

The bride graduated _____
Include honors such as summa cum laude, etc., if applicable

from _____, where she received her
Name of College/University

_____ in _____. She is also a
Cite Degree Subject of Degree/Major

graduate of _____, where she received her
Name of College/University

_____ in _____.
Cite Degree Subject of Degree/Major

The groom graduated _____
Include honors such as summa cum laude, etc., if applicable

from _____, where he received his
Name of College/University

_____ in _____. He is also a
Cite Degree Subject of Degree/Major

graduate of _____, where he received his
Name of College/University

_____ in _____.
Cite Degree Subject of Degree/Major

Ms. /Dr._____ is the daughter of
Bride's Name

_____ of _____. Her father is a
Names of Bride's Parents City/State Where Parents Reside

_____. Her mother is a
Name of Profession or Retired Profession

_____.
Name of Profession or Retired Profession

Mr./Dr. _____ is the son of _____ of
Groom's Name Names of Groom's Parents

_____. His father is a
City/State Where Groom's Parents Reside

_____. His mother is a _____ .
Name of Profession or Retired Profession Name of Profession or Retired Profession

A _____wedding is planned in
Month of Wedding

_____. The couple plans to reside in
City/State Where Wedding Will Be Held

_____.
City/State Where You Plan to Live

For more information, please contact:

_____
Bride or Groom's Name

_____
Address

_____
Work Phone

_____
Home Phone

_____
E-mail

How to Word Your Wedding Invitation

If the traditional wording on pages 34 and 35 doesn't suit your needs, consider one of these:

Parents Co-Hosting

Mr. and Mrs. Matthew James Hayden
and Mr. and Mrs. William Stanley Banks
request the honour of your presence
at the marriage of their children
Victoria Lynn
and
Kyle William
Saturday, the ninth of September
Two thousand and six
at half after three o'clock
St. Thomas Church
Springfield, Massachusetts

Bride, Groom, and Parents Co-Hosting

Victoria Lynn Hayden
and
Kyle William Banks
together with their parents,
Mr. and Mrs. Matthew James Hayden
and Mr. and Mrs. William Stanley Banks,
request the honour of your presence
at their marriage
Saturday, the ninth of September
Two thousand and six
at half after three o'clock
St. Thomas Church
Springfield, Massachusetts

Divorced Parents—Bride's Side

Mrs. Katherine Hayden
[or Mrs. Steven Green, if she is remarried]
and
Mr. Matthew James Hayden
request the honour of your presence
at the marriage of their daughter
Victoria Lynn
to
Kyle William Banks
Saturday, the ninth of September
Two thousand and six
at half after three o'clock
St. Thomas Church
Springfield, Massachusetts

Divorced Parents—Groom's Side

Mr. and Mrs. Matthew James Hayden
request the honour of your presence
at the marriage of their daughter
Victoria Lynn
to
Kyle William Banks
son of
Mrs. Deborah Banks
and
Mr. William Stanley Banks
Saturday, the ninth of September
Two thousand and six
at half after three o'clock
St. Thomas Church
Springfield, Massachusetts

Remarried Parents

Mr. and Mrs. Anthony Ryder [Bride's mother
and stepfather]
and
Mr. and Mrs. Matthew James Hayden [Bride's father
and stepmother]
request the honour of your presence
at the marriage of their daughter
Victoria Lynn
to
Kyle William Banks
Saturday, the ninth of September
Two thousand and six
at half after three o'clock
St. Thomas Church
Springfield, Massachusetts

OR

Ms. Katherine Hayden [Bride's mother]
and
Mr. and Mrs. Matthew James Hayden [Bride's father
and stepmother]
request the honour of your presence
at the marriage of their daughter
Victoria Lynn
to
Kyle William Banks
Saturday, the ninth of September
Two thousand and six
at half after three o'clock
St. Thomas Church
Springfield, Massachusetts

Several Sets of Parents Hosting

The loving parents of
Victoria Lynn Hayden
and
Kyle William Banks
request the honour of your presence
at the marriage of their children
Saturday, the ninth of September
Two thousand and six
at half after three o'clock
St. Thomas Church
Springfield, Massachusetts

Single Parent with Live-in Partner

Mrs. Katherine Hayden [Bride's mother]
and
Mr. Walter Reed [Live-in Partner]
request the honour of your presence
at the marriage of
Mrs. Hayden's daughter
Victoria Lynn
to
Kyle William Banks
Saturday, the ninth of September
Two thousand and six
at half after three o'clock
St. Thomas Church
Springfield, Massachusetts

Bride and Groom Hosting

Victoria Lynn Hayden
and
Kyle William Banks
request the honour of your presence
at their marriage
Saturday, the ninth of September
Two thousand and six
at half after three o'clock
St. Thomas Church
Springfield, Massachusetts

Deceased Parent

Mrs. Matthew James Hayden
requests the honour of your presence
at the marriage of her daughter
Victoria Lynn
to
Kyle William Banks
Saturday, the ninth of September
Two thousand and six
at half after three o'clock
St. Thomas Church
Springfield, Massachusetts

OR

Together with their families,
Victoria Lynn Hayden,
daughter of Matthew James Hayden and the late
Katherine Hayden,
and

Kyle William Banks,
son of Mr. and Mrs. William Stanley Banks,
request the honour of your presence
at their marriage
Saturday, the ninth of September
Two thousand and six
at half after three o'clock
St. Thomas Church
Springfield, Massachusetts

OR

The honour of your presence is requested at the
marriage of
Victoria Lynn Hayden,
daughter of Matthew James Hayden and the late
Katherine Hayden
to
Kyle William Banks,
son of Mr. and Mrs. William Stanley Banks,
Saturday, the ninth of September
Two thousand and six
at half after three o'clock
St. Thomas Church
Springfield, Massachusetts

Relative Hosting

Mr. and Mrs. Joshua Prince
request the honour of your presence
at the marriage of their niece
Victoria Lynn Hayden
to
Kyle William Banks

Saturday, the ninth of September
Two thousand and six
at half after three o'clock
St. Thomas Church
Springfield, Massachusetts

Bride's Second Marriage

Mr. and Mrs. Matthew James Hayden
request the honour of your presence
at the marriage of their daughter
Victoria Lynn Peters
to
Kyle William Banks
Saturday, the ninth of September
Two thousand and six
at half after three o'clock
St. Thomas Church
Springfield, Massachusetts

Bride and/or Groom with Doctoral Title

Mr. and Mrs. Matthew James Hayden
request the honour of your presence
at the marriage of their daughter
Doctor Victoria Lynn Hayden
to
Doctor Kyle William Banks
Saturday, the ninth of September
Two thousand and six
at half after three o'clock
St. Thomas Church
Springfield, Massachusetts

Military Titles

Colonel (Ret.) and Mrs. Matthew James Hayden
request the honour of your presence
at the marriage of their daughter
Victoria Lynn
Lieutenant, United States Army
to
Colonel Kyle William Banks
United States Army
Saturday, the ninth of September
Two thousand and six
at half after three o'clock
St. Thomas Church
Springfield, Massachusetts

More on Military Titles

The use of military titles can be confusing to the uninitiated. Here are a few guidelines to keep in mind:

- The title of an officer whose rank is equal to or higher than a captain in the army is placed before the name with the branch of the service on the line below.

    Colonel Kyle William Banks
    United States Army

- The title of an officer whose rank is equal to or higher than a lieutenant in the navy is placed before the name with the branch of the service on the line below.

    Lieutenant Michael Grand
    United States Navy

- For lower-ranking members of the military, the rank and branch of the service are listed together below the name.

Michael Grand
Ensign, United States Navy

- Indicate (Ret.) after the title of a high-ranking officer who is retired.

Appendix B: Religious Rituals and Traditions

Interested in learning more about your own religious rituals or those of your fiancé? Here's the basics on eight common traditions.

Buddhist

Buddhism has many sects, which have varying ways of performing a wedding ceremony. In addition to the religious aspects of Buddhism, the couple's country or countries of origin can determine what the bride and groom wear and what cultural rituals are part of the ceremony.

Many Buddhist wedding ceremonies—which may be held either in a temple or outdoors—take place in a *poruwa*, a platform beneath a white silk canopy that symbolizes the couple's new home. The canopy is usually covered in white flowers, and flowerpots are placed on each corner of the platform. Often there is an altar with a statue of Buddha and two lighted candles: one for the couple and one for the community at large.

A Buddhist-ordained clergy member—often a monk—presides over the ceremony, which begins and ends with the ringing of bells to symbolize purification. Early in the ceremony, the couple bow to the altar, light the two candles, and place flowers on the altar as an offering. Then the presider may anoint the ground with water (if the ceremony is held outdoors) or pour water into a bowl of flowers (if the ceremony is held indoors) to symbolize purity, beauty, love, and compassion. After the couple recites vows and exchanges wedding rings, the celebrant may perform hand fasting, in which he loosely binds the hands of the bride and groom together with a sash of silk (different cultures use different colors—often white or red) or a Buddhist rosary. In some cases, he then pours water over the couple's joined hands. In some cultures, the bride and groom share betel leaves with their parents as a sign of respect. Finally, the truths taught by Buddha are read aloud and the ceremony concludes with the ringing of bells.

Eastern Orthodox

The Eastern Orthodox wedding ceremony, which in some ways is similar to the Roman Catholic ceremony, includes a Gospel reading as well as several rituals performed three times each to represent the Holy Trinity: the Father, the son, and the Holy Spirit. These rituals include the blessing and exchange of rings, the placing of crowns on the heads of the bride and the groom, and the sharing of a cup of wine. During the crown ritual, the priest or a male godparent exchanges crowns between the bride's and groom's head three times to symbolize the crowning glory of God and to signify that the bride and groom are to be king and queen in their own home. The crowns are bound together with a long cord that signifies the couple's unity and commitment to each other. Wearing the crowns, the couple walks around the altar three times, following the priest who carries a large, ornate Bible, as the congregation sings "God Grant Them Many Years." These are the couple's first steps together as husband and wife.

Hindu

The ceremony for a Hindu wedding can vary depending on where in India a family is from and where the wedding is taking place. Generally, the main ceremony lasts about two and a half hours, though including the preliminary rituals and events after the ceremony, the wedding can last from three to seven days. One of the preparation rituals is *mendhi*—in which the bride's hands and feet are decorated with beautiful henna designs by the women in her family. For the ceremony, the bride usually wears a *sari* in red or pink and is adorned with many pieces of jewelry around her head, hands, and feet.

A Hindu ceremony can take place in any covered area, but it is usually held under a tent-like wedding pavilion called a *mandap*. The mandap is a 7- to 9-foot-tall canopy with a cloth-covered top decorated with flowers and greenery and supported by nine large wooden poles. The mandap represents the universe and the nine poles represent the nine planets. Within the mandap, there is usually an altar and seats for the bride and groom.

In many cases, the ceremony is performed completely in Sanskrit.

The most important ceremony ritual is *sapta-padi*, in which the couple recites seven vows as they take seven steps together around a fire that's lighted before the ceremony and dedicated to the fire god Agni to symbolize purity and the eternal flame of love. This is symbolic of the couple's journey through life together. According to ancient Hindu mythology, the sapta-padi represent wishes for seven things: food, strength, wealth, happiness, children, cattle, and devotion. Some couples also circle the fire four times—with the groom leading the bride two times and the bride leading the groom two times—to symbolize religion, prosperity, family, and unity with God. Often the couple's families throw rice and flowers into the fire as an offering to God.

Other rituals that may be part of the ceremony include the exchange of garlands by the bride and groom to signify that they accept the marriage and the marking of the bride's forehead with red powder to symbolize her new life as a married woman. Sometimes the bride's parents place her hand in the groom's and pour water on the hands to show that the family no longer has ties to her. In some Hindu sects, the groom places a beaded chain around the bride's neck to signify love, devotion and marriage. At the end of many Hindu wedding ceremonies, family members sprinkle rose petals, symbolic of blessings, on the couple.

Jewish

When it comes to wedding ceremony traditions, there are some differences between the Orthodox, Conservative, Reform, and Reconstructionist branches of Judaism, so couples should speak with their rabbi to determine the correct practices for their wedding. One common element is that Jewish wedding ceremonies take place under a wedding canopy called a huppah (or chuppah) that is symbolic of the home the couple will share. The huppah is usually made of fabric (and may be decorated with greenery or flowers) and is supported by four poles (representing the four corners of the earth), which are held by the ushers or other honored guests. The bride, groom, their parents, the rabbi, and the bridal party all stand beneath the huppah.

Jewish weddings cannot take place on the Sabbath, during Passover, or on other holy days. Most take place after sundown on Saturdays or on Sundays. The wedding ceremonies can take place in a synagogue or temple or in another location such as a hotel or reception venue. Most ceremonies are performed in English and Hebrew, though a strict Orthodox ceremony is usually entirely in Hebrew.

During the service, the bride circles around the groom either three or seven times (both are considered mystical numbers; three because a husband has three obligations—food, clothing, and conjugal relationships—and seven for the number of days it took God to create the universe) and the couple shares sanctified wine from a kiddush cup, which symbolizes the cup of life. The couple also exchanges vows and rings. The exchange of rings is very important, because in Jewish law a declaration of marriage is not binding until a ring or something else of nominal value is given to the bride by the groom. For the Jewish ceremony, plain gold bands are placed on the index finger, which was traditionally believed to lead directly to the heart. A marriage contract called a *ketubah* is read (the couple usually signs the ketubah, a framed document, before the ceremony and hangs it in their home after the wedding) and the rabbi recites the Seven Blessings (also known as the Seven Benedictions), which give thanks for the occasion and offer wishes for the bride and groom. Some couples ask family members or close friends to recite some of the blessings. The rabbi then offers a closing blessing and the groom breaks a glass by stomping on it and the entire congregation shouts "Mazel Tov"—which means congratulations and good luck. The breaking of the glass symbolizes several things: the destruction of the temple in Israel, the fragility of life, and the fact that marriage is a transformative experience and the couple will never be the same. After the ceremony, the newlyweds spend fifteen minutes in private (this is known as *yichud*) before they emerge for the reception celebration.

Muslim

Some Muslim wedding ceremonies are held in mosques, but the ceremony can also take place in a home, wedding hall, courtroom, or office where the couple signs the marriage contract. The Muslim ceremony itself is only about five minutes long, but many ceremonies also include cultural traditions that are based on the couple's countries of origin. For example, there are additional rituals that are specific to Moroccan weddings, Iranian weddings, and so on.

Muslim ceremonies are usually presided over by an *imam*, an Islamic religious leader. In addition, there must be two witnesses to oversee the written and oral contract between the bride and the groom. The bride and groom are each asked if they are happy with the arrangement and if they agree to marry the other, and the groom gives the bride a dower—something of monetary value such as a ring, money, or property—to symbolize that he is assuming responsibility for the family they are forming. Most ceremonies include a variety of prayers and blessings, and they always include a reading of the Koran by the imam. Sometimes a white cloth is placed on the bride and groom's heads or hands and the Koran is held above the cloth. This symbolizes God's protection and purity.

In some traditions, the men and women present for the ceremony (including the bride and groom) sit in separate areas or are separated by a curtain.

Protestant

Within the Protestant Church there are many denominations, including Amish, Baptist, Episcopal, Lutheran, and Mormon, and the procedures and order of rituals for each vary accordingly. In general, the Protestant wedding ceremony is a fairly short service based on the Book of Common Prayer. The service begins with opening words (also called welcoming words) by the minister and a reading from the Bible (this may be done by a family member or special guest), the couple's declaration of intent to marry, and the exchange of vows and rings. In some congregations, there is also a congregational vow of support, in which the minister asks those gathered if they support this union and the congregation answers "We do." After the vows and rings, the couple may light a unity candle that symbolizes the light of their marriage. The minister then offers prayers for the couple's future and the couple may share a cup of wine. Finally, the minister offers a Benediction or closing blessing and pronounces the couple married.

Roman Catholic

There are two options when it comes to a Roman Catholic wedding. You can choose a nuptial mass that includes the Liturgy of the Word and the Liturgy of the Eucharist, and lasts from forty-five minutes to one hour. Or you can opt for a non-mass ceremony that is shorter since it eliminates the Liturgy of the Eucharist.

Catholic ceremonies can be held on most any date—except the holy days around Easter including Holy Thursday, Good Friday, and Holy Saturday—as long as the ceremony doesn't interfere with the weekend mass schedule.

The components of a Catholic nuptial mass include: the introductory rites (the greeting by the priest), the Liturgy of the Word (reading the selected scriptures), the priest's homily, the couples' declaration of consent, the vows, the blessing and exchange of rings, the Liturgy of the Eucharist, and the concluding rite. Some couples choose to present flowers to the mothers of the bride and groom during the sign of peace. Additionally, some couples lay a small bouquet of flowers in front of the Virgin Mary during the ceremony.

Shinto

Shinto, which means the way of the gods, is a religion practiced by many Japanese people. A Shinto wedding ceremony takes place in a Shinto shrine or chapel, and is presided over by a Shinto priest.

During the ceremony, the priest says prayers and the couple exchange rings and take part in an important ritual called *sakazukigoto* or *sansankudo,* which is done in silence. In this the bride and groom each drink from three flat cups of sake (rice wine)—small, medium, and large—that are stacked on top of each other. The groom takes three sips from a cup and then passes it to the bride so she can take three sips, and they repeat the process with the other two cups. Drinking from the small cup represents giving thanks to their ancestors; the medium cup symbolizes a promise to live and work together for the rest of their lives; and the large cup represents the couple's prayer for a happy home filled with children. After the bride and groom take their sips, the sake is offered to the groom's father, the groom's mother, the bride's father, and the bride's mother.

Sometimes the priest will wave a wand made of strips of white paper to symbolize purification. The final ritual is the offering of *tamagushi,* or sacred leaves, by the bride and groom. The couple places the tamagushi at the altar to represent contact between humans and kami or spirits. Finally, the priest offers a prayer and congratulates the couple.

❧ Acknowledgments ☙

Many people generously shared their knowledge and expertise to make this book complete. Special thanks to Barry Rosenbloom, Yelena Malinovskaya, Lisa Dickens, and Cybele Eidenschenk from *Bridal Guide*. Also thanks to wedding planners Lois Pearce of Beautiful Occasions in Hamden, Connecticut, and Karen Erwin of St. Augustine Weddings and Special Events in St. Augustine, Florida, as well as Reverend Susanna Stefanachi Macomb, author of *Joining Hands and Heart: Interfaith, Intercultural Wedding Celebrations*; Anna Mehta of The Dream Planners in New Jersey; Rabbi Eric Milgrim of Temple B'nai Shalom in East Brunswick, New Jersey; Dana Finello; Denise Dinyon, bridal and special events manager for Lenox Brands; Roseanna Robinson, national bridal director for Pfaltzgraff; Gary Marr, senior director of catering at the Hyatt Regency Chicago; and Rebecca Tushnet, assistant professor of law at New York University School of Law. And thanks to Melanie Murray, Amy Einhorn, and Anna Maria Piluso from Warner Books, and Jacqueline Grace, Cathy Repetti, Megan Gilbert, and Amy Wilson from LifeTime Media, Inc.

Index

M

maid/matron of honor. *See also* bridal party
asking mother to be, 8
difference between maid and matron, 12
role and responsibilities of, 19, 76–78
selecting, 9

maiden name, and announcing husband and wife, 143

maps and directions, including with invitation, 40

marriage ceremony. *See* ceremony, marriage

marriage license, 128–130

meal, reception, 133–135, 144
for destination weddings, 198

memories, invoking, for renewing vows, 232–233

men's wedding attire, 90–91

military titles, using in invitations, 287–288

mother of the bride
asking to be matron of honor, 8
conflicts with, 250–251
gift ideas for, 65
role and responsibilities of, 70–71

mother of the groom
gift ideas for, 65
and mother-son dance, 146
role and responsibilities of, 73–74

music
for ceremony, 106
and hiring musicians, 107
live versus prerecorded, 107

Muslim traditions, 294

N

newlywed life, enjoying, 269

newsletter, wedding, 77

newspaper, engagement
announcements in, 3
for second marriages, 208–209

O

office co-workers
throwing bridal showers, 25
whether to invite, 49, 251

officiant
for destination weddings, 197
working with, 104–105

online registries, 160–161

open bar, versus cash bar, 135

P

parents. *See* bride's parents; groom's parents

parties, pre-wedding, 17–29. *See also* specific parties (i.e. bridal shower, bachelor party, etc.)

party, bridal. *See* bridal party

place cards, 141–142

postponement, wedding, 166, 256–257

pregnant bridesmaids, 80

printing options, for invitations, 32–33

procession, order of, 112–113

programs, wedding, 117–122

Protestant rituals and traditions, 294–295